You Are Love

Christianity Transformed

and

The New Message of Love

by Sue Kidd Shipe, PhD.

"Moriah", A Teacher of Love

You Are Love
Christianity Transformed

You Are Love: Christianity Transformed provides a way for Christians, current and former, those who are "done" with religion, and those who identify as "spiritual but not religious" to reignite their faith and expand their abilities in alignment with their spiritual purpose.

The New Message of Love is given to Humanity to help it safely navigate the rapid changes of the New World. The New Message of Love is for all of all faiths, or none, and is also the next step in human spiritual understanding and evolution. The skills learned in The New Message of Love are relevant to all. They are the next step in the transformation of Christianity.

This intervention comes to Humanity as it prepares to navigate the changes brought by this New World.

Dedicated to the Provider of Unseen Assistance

'A New Way for a New Day!'
New World Empowerment Center
www.newworldempowerment.com
www.humanempowerment.org

Published by the International Institute For Human Empowerment, Inc.

Copyright 2022   All rights reserved.

ISBN: 978-0-9709461-5-7

You Are Love
Christianity Transformed

You Are Love

Christianity Transformed

You Are Love
Christianity Transformed

You Are Love

If you're a Christian, you know. The stressors are all around. You turn to your faith, and often it is the difference between complete despair, and inexplicable peace. At other times, you may feel disillusioned. Alone. Uncertain. Skeptical. Unsure. Rudderless. Angry. Afraid.

If you are feeling disillusioned and confused, you are not alone. The "Nones" are those who report themselves as "spiritual but not religious", agnostic, and atheist. The "Dones" are those who were often previously very active in their respective religions, but have despaired, and left dissatisfied. Compared with those who identify as Evangelical, Catholic, or Protestant, the "Nones" and the "Dones" are outpacing those groups who identify with religion. You need only to see the shuttered churches, and church buildings converted to places of business or residence, to witness the effect. However, if you are becoming disillusioned, this statistic may only serve to increase your sense of isolation and distrust.

If you are comforted, and your important questions are answered, you are becoming unique. Thousands, millions, are looking for more. More relevance to their daily lives. More inclusiveness; less judging. More compatibility between faith and science. More respect for the individual as a whole person with less focus on sin. More openness to questioning. More integrity in behavior at all levels. More open minds. More respect for differences. More trust; less control. More focus on preservation of the earth and all within. More flexibility in primary relationships in order to meet the needs of both people. More recognition of the value of the human spirit. More respect for all loving spiritual paths. More focus on forgiveness and less on revenge. More open-minded and relevant interpretation of the Bible for the time in which we are living. More respect for healing modalities that complement traditional therapies. More respect for individual needs. More support for the family in its many expressions. More value of service over acquisition. More concern for human and animal suffering. More respect for individual differences, including unexplained experiences. More desire to make one's spirituality the center of one's life. More sense of purpose. More sense of security. More understanding of the value of each individual person as an expression of Love.

It is OK to question. It is OK to explore other paths. It is OK to be open-minded to scientific exploration. It is OK to meditate. It is OK to incorporate one's unexplained experiences into one's spirituality. It is OK to see oneself and others as spiritual beings expressing in human form. It is OK to explore the many expressions of energy, and their meaning. It is OK to continue to learn. And, it is OK to incorporate these new learnings into what we might call, "The Empowered Christian," or "Christianity Transformed!"

This spiritually empowered Christian accepts that when Jesus came as God incarnate, He intended that we do likewise. How? That's what this book will attempt to show you. Don't wait any longer for the Second Coming. It is here. It is now. It is humans accepting that they are spiritual beings, constantly expanding their consciousness to incorporate more Love energy, known as God. It is Jesus saying, "Do as I do." He became Love incarnate, that we might also evolve to become carriers of that same Love energy that He carried. That Love energy empowered Him to be able to hear without words; see beyond the body to the soul to know what was in a person's heart, or intent; heal with energy and loving intent; lead with integrity; love without boundaries; and love without judgment. It is what He commanded us to do. To love thy neighbor as thyself requires the highest level of love vibration. To heal is to harness the energy of love and apply it to deficits, known and unrecognized. To lead with integrity is to choose love in all decisions. The manifestation of Love is love.

Now it's your turn. Give yourself permission to explore. Trust that God loves you as you are including doubts, fears, and distractions. Believe that if Jesus loved you to the Cross, that He loves you beyond it. Believe that God is active in the energy of our world, expressing in caring actions, defending against oppression, and healing in and beyond the body. Recognize that spiritual empowerment is the living expression of Love energy acting in our world today. Be a part of moving that Love energy more broadly so that more are cared for, healed, and loved. Recognize that as an individual person you have the capacity to carry Love energy in the world. You have the capacity to choose to become spiritually empowered. And know that as each of us, regardless of belief or spiritual path, carries that Love energy in the world, our world will change. Energy flows through us, moves us, moves beyond us, and impacts those around us and beyond.

Imagine light. It shines upon all. It does not distinguish between good and bad. It does not judge. It is there: powerful, penetrating, exposing, recognizing. Now think of Love. It is an energy that surrounds and is in us. It can appear to dissipate, then be harnessed for power. It is all inclusive. It expresses through humans and animals. It comforts when distressed. It heals the sick and broken-hearted. It serves others in a multitude of ways. It is there in the beginning, and at the passing on of life. It is always there, waiting for our recognition and integration.

This is not about being saved or damned. It is about accepting that we already are a part of Love. It is recognizing that when we leave this world, it will be with the energy and light with which we came and live. We are already "saved." We need only to recognize it. Everything we already need is here; we need only to access it. When we pray, we ask; when we meditate or listen, we receive.

Now life has meaning because we are one with One. We are energetic beings, harnessing Love energy, sharing it with others, and emitting a powerful energy into the universe. As our consciousness expands with Love, so we change our world. Like the wind, we may not see it, but we can feel and see the effects. We are Love in the world when we choose to harness the energy of Love for good.

You Are Love: Christianity Transformed, including **The New Message of Love**, is relevant to today. It provides spiritual practice, and current and broader perspective, while incorporating one's personal and unique experiences. It is for the believer, the non-believer, and the one searching. It is the next step in humanity's spiritual evolution. Through accepting the **Invitation to Love**, and doing the year-long course of study called **Journey to Love**, you will find that you have accessed the energy of Love and become Spiritually Empowered.

All of life is the Healing Journey. Each person's journey is part of the human experience, yet unique. It is only in later life, as we look back, that we can see that the journey of life is the healing Journey to Love.

Do not be afraid. You are already loved, cared for, and protected. Accept only those relationships that cherish and support you, so that you may flourish. Take Christianity to a new level by becoming Spiritually Empowered, so that you may be Love in the world.

May everything you do be done for Love.

—Moriah

You Are Love
Christianity Transformed

Contents

You Are Love

Forward: You Are Love	7
Introduction	15
1. Christianity Transformed is The New Christianity	21
2. Taking Our Religion to a New Level	31
3. Inspired by Change, or Changed by Inspiration?	36
4. It's a New World Requiring an Empowered Faith	43
5. Receiving the Invitation	47
6. Taking the Journey	55
7. From Pain to Gain	59
8. The New Christian	67
9. Healed! Empowered!	71
10. Ready to Lead Change	77
11. Be the Change!	81
Transition	84
New World Definitions	85

The New Message of Love   91

	I.	Invitation to Love	97
	II.	Journey to Love	255
	III.	The Healing Journey	399

Resources	503
Index: Inspirations	504

Introduction

Transformed Through Spiritual Empowerment

You are Love. You may not be aware yet, but you are being uncovered. Your values are morphing. Your desires are changing. You are drawn to some people, activities, and beliefs, and away from others. The outside world is changing rapidly, and that is being mirrored internally. Life as you have understood it is about to take a giant leap forward. What you may have only wondered about is taking shape. How you see yourself is undergoing rapid transformation. Do not try to hold onto the past; it is gone. Prepare now for the future that is arriving.

It's a New Day! Memories of childhood long forgotten may arise only to reinforce what you have always known. What you know is much different from what you've been taught. Nothing is as you once believed. Change is constant, and what was, is gone. What has arrived is life-granting, recognizable, integrated, and full of Love.

Forget what you believed. You are lovable. You can learn to see through deceit and dishonesty. You are capable of so much more than you believe. You have the capacity to see, hear, feel, sense, and know far more than you have believed. Now it is time to develop new awareness, open your mind to new information, remove man-made illusions, and begin to see your capacity to expand and grow as limitless.

You do not need to be saved because you are evil, but you do need to be saved from the judgments of others. You will emerge from the death of a physical body to the pure light and love that you are.

If this promise seems too large, expand your ability to be open to a new reality—a new reality of you. You are Love. You need only to be open and allow for this power to transform you. Love (God) transforms. It can be no other way.

The transformation to the new and empowered person is also the transformation of Christianity. When we examine the life of Jesus Christ in the context of the New World, His relevance is greater even than before. Do not miss this life-enhancing opportunity due to your limiting beliefs! His life is much more than a history book. It is the vital life force called Love that permeates our lives.

Yet all of this is nothing without your active preparation. You may stumble upon special moments and insights, randomly following a path that you have designed. Or, you may choose the Preparation in Journey to Love to take you to spiritual empowerment directly.

You will arrive in the New World, but will you arrive prepared?

The Color of Love

Jesus, would I paint you,
    What colors should I choose
To show how long you suffered
    To prepare your life to lose?

The blackest black of darkest night
    Could never yet portray
The depth of passion, oft forgot,
    When You one did betray.

What shading should I use for fear,
    That thunder in the heart
That roars like crashing surf on sand
    When with life we would part?

Yet, but another color
    For the sadness and the pain
Of leaving those you loved behind
    Eternal life to gain.

No, I would paint you yellow,
    As vivid as the sun above,
To show the brilliance and the power
    Of your greatest attribute, Love.

In Their Voices

'Behold, I bring you good tidings of great joy!'   (Luke 2:10)

>The Christ child was born!
>A new era began that day.
>Christianity was born.
>And so it was.

The 21st century marks over 2000 years since our Leader, Jesus Christ, was born. The world into which Jesus was born little resembles our world today. As disillusionment, and increased desire for more relevance became apparent, a New Message arrived to help us safely navigate the New World. This is the era of You Are Love: Christianity Transformed!

>2000 years have passed.
>The world changed.
>The struggle for relevance in Christianity is real!

With this new interpretation of Jesus' words, and addition of The New Message of Love, Christianity now has deeper meaning and more relevance for today.

Before you abandon your heritage, consider this contemporary interpretation. You'll find new answers to age-old questions, and a path toward inner peace.

When the world grew dark, a new intervention was sent to guide us. Christianity now resonates with new life and meaning through this new revelation!

You Are Love: Christianity Transformed and **The New Message of Love** have been given to humanity by Angels through Moriah. Here is the Message in their voices…

…Love is the Source of all true empowerment. That is the same today as over 2000 years ago. What is different now is that the Energy of Love that came into the world is now universally available for every person who chooses. The choice does not need to be emotional, but it must be sincere. There can be no pretending, as those who have become empowered with Love Energy can recognize pretense. It must be a clear, honest, conscious choice. The choice must be made by each individual everywhere.

21st Century—Pandemics, revelations of intelligent life not of the earth entering our airspace, fires, floods, rapidly morphing temperatures, air that is not safe to breathe and water that is unsafe to drink. Much has occurred; much more will continue to happen. The results of environmental abuse combined with planetary changes are making the planet and its inhabitants ill. New viruses, allergies, and neurological challenges are wreaking havoc with healthcare systems which must continually change in order to remain effective.

Those who choose not to accept the energy of Love will add to the current chaos. Out of lack of understanding, they hold fast to that which can no longer save them. Their intuition, needed to navigate the world, has become hidden by social lies and expectations. Their once open hearts are shut in anger and fear. Their lifestyles are frantic even as they market products and t soothe. They are dangerous because they are not ... hey are not centered. They scream that they have answer... ile inwardly being terrified that they have none. They pretend to have answers, and fear being disloyal for asking questions. Those who interpret without a broader context for understanding, claim their right to self-righteousness.

Love Energy will challenge all who feel steeped in the answers given by their religion. If they can be open to new information, they will be able to grow and build upon the past, rather that destroy it. Love Energy will provide the next step in their spiritual evolution.

This will be a time of unity, or of great division. Love Energy will pull all toward It. Those who cannot accept will be left behind. Be most cautious of all who reject, as they may become violent while intending to preserve the past.

The previous Message was given for the past. The past is gone. Love Energy is here and will move all who accept into broader understanding and acceptance. They will learn to receive direct guidance.

Love is universal, available to all, yet also personal. It brings together all who can accept. It allows those who are unable, to remain. It is a sad and painful time, yet essential as your planet's intelligent life makes contact and joins with the Others, non- human intelligences. Love Energy is what will allow you to recognize motives in order to remain safe.

Chapter 1

Christianity Transformed is The New Christianity

The New Christianity is founded upon a Preparation that expands upon the Teachings of Jesus Christ through the addition of Experience. This Preparation is called, "The New Message of Love." The New Christianity moves beyond faith to incorporate new Experiences, many of which do not fit our current paradigm of reality. The result is The New Christianity, a spiritual life of Faith plus Experience.

Current structures based upon faith alone continue to struggle to survive. Now, an expanded view of Jesus' Teachings may be found in The New Message of Love. As religious structures continue to face growing challenges, The New Christianity is breathing new life into Christianity by:

1) expanding interpretations of Jesus' teachings of love to be relevant to a New World;
2) enhancing faith alone by adding one's personal anomalous experiences.

This allows one to become a Channel for Love. Here one moves from believing in the power of love, to being Love in the world.

Love is vibrational energy. Everything is energy in motion called vibrations. Love is the attainment of a high level of energy, while fear remains at the lowest levels of vibration. One can see Love and Fear expressing in the actions taken by oneself and others. Jesus was Love Incarnate. The devil is a representation of low-level vibrations: hurtful; destructive; uncaring, even horrific, actions. Our lives are on the spectrum between Love and fear. Our desire as Christians is to follow Jesus in order to be Love in the world.

What does it mean to "Be Love in the World"? It means to emanate Love energy which is attained through surrender to Love, the power or force of creation, and by allowing It to be your guide. Decisions, spiritual paths, and relationships, exist following guidance from Beyond.

Christians often speak of morality, or the voice inside, giving direction, opposing some choices, and approving of others. The moral compass is known within The New Christianity as Intuition.

All animals are intuitive. They know. They know when to mate, when to migrate, how to raise and protect their young, and how to avoid predators. Intuition is part of the Consciousness that is passed from generation to generation. However, this form of Intuition in The New Christianity is even more profound, as it can be accessed directly for Guidance. This Guidance becomes consciously available through surrendering of our will, or ego, to the will of God, or the Creator. Through surrender, we give up our small mind, or ego self, in order to attain broader vision and understanding through this greater mind.

Love is spoken of by poets, lovers, families, and friends, and is the ideal for all of our relationships. However, relationships developed for spiritual purpose are an even higher level of love, and support the participants mutually through the challenges of their spiritual journey. Relationships may initially be ignited through romantic love, but the aspect of knowing one is with the right partner for oneself is only found through profound Intuition.

The Teaching of Jesus changed the world. For over 2000 years, it has provided peace, protection, security, direction, hope, joy, and a way to live one's life. It will continue into the future, guiding our steps within the familiar. However, during the radical shifts of the 21st century, new challenges have arisen that require us to look Beyond for more assistance. How will we navigate rapid change? How will we find stability during erratic shifts within our climate; governments; philosophies; beliefs; health challenges including pandemics; as well as mixing of cultures, languages, and appearances? Perhaps even more notable, our individual and collective world view of what constitutes "reality" is no longer viable.

Around the globe, people are experiencing events, both personal and collective, that defy our understanding. A counter-culture has developed and expanded rapidly, where those having unique and unexplained experiences can find comfort in the presence of others with similar unusual events. Many have found comfort and safe surroundings through the use of social media to meet privately with others.

Where there are no answers, people seek comfort. They seek direction. They follow others who proclaim to have deeper understanding, and too often are used for others' advantage. How do I know what's real? What can I trust? Who can I trust? How can I trust?

Perhaps the biggest liability of our rapidly changing times is loss of trust in our institutions. The media, designed to keep us a free people through exposing injustices, has become political. The justice system claims to be fair, but has too often proven otherwise through patterns of discrimination that have been condoned by the masses. Schools designed to teach our children to think critically and derive the knowledge, skills, and character to become successful adults, fall too often to political pressure, losing sight of their mission.

Our healthcare has expanded so quickly that research is too often ignored for expediency. In an ever-changing science, the practitioner must stay abreast of new information, or fail to treat patients effectively with the dignity and concern required.

The critical measure of each political leader needs to be caring of all whom they represent. Favoritism, inappropriate use of funds, and unlawful behaviors have been too often demonstrated by those who promised to serve. It has caused government failure to thrive due to mistrust of leaders and the decisions they make.

Change is a constant, and has always been. However, with the explosion of technology, the world has shrunk. People, products, and lifestyles we would never have known existed are now a part of our everyday lives. So, when we start hearing more about events that don't fit society's generally accepted idea of reality, that information spreads quickly and can no longer be contained.

Millions of people around the world have come together in chat rooms and private groups on social media. Here, many have revealed deeply troubling secrets to those with whom they feel "safe." The rapid expansion of social media, and its many uses, have allowed people to gather with others who would never be known without technology. These groups have expanded exponentially, while attendance in traditional religious services has diminished.

We don't have to look far to establish one of the chief causes of this shift. Relevance. Many attempts have been and are being made daily to apply Christian ideals to a world that little resembles the world in the time of Jesus. Traditions that have served generations are considered outdated by many. The ability to gather is no longer limited by proximity. Technology gives us access, and allows for assembly globally. Ideas travel fast. Traditions morph. Values shift. Customs blend. Religions with rules to prevent interaction with others of differing beliefs are being challenged as people assimilate parts of other cultures and practices, and live in a world where travel opens up unlimited possibilities.

No longer do we sleep and work according to the sun. No longer is learning limited to schools and colleges, as information can be accessed from anywhere.

No longer are people accepting the advice of experts without researching other options. No longer are experts given deference, but are treated without regard for degrees and experience.

No longer do people think they want experts, while desperately seeking answers. People want leadership, but they may have forgotten how to trust.

When the clerics can't give answers that satisfy; when churches are focused on doctrine and cannot allow for exceptions; when new information contradicts long-held beliefs; when people are confused and scared; where can they go? The old falls away if it cannot be responsive to new and growing needs. Can religion as we know it address those needs? Or, must religion expand, and become open to new ideas, in order to be relevant in a rapidly changing world experiencing disruption in every area?

Consider the lives of your grandparents and parents. Consider your youth. Consider the world your children will live in as adults.

When we were young, most of us had something we trusted. We believed: in education, media, medicine, government, and business. Now ask yourself whom you trust.

The New World we live in is a model of simultaneous change in every aspect: personal, professional, spiritual, academic, communications, politics, weather. What hasn't changed is the human need for love, security, belonging, something to believe in, and something worthwhile to contribute. We are Christians, but those who seek connection to a Higher Source must open their minds to examine and contemplate the meaning of life and their foundation for trust.

What can we trust as the institutions we have believed and clung to are crumbling? How do we find security when all of life feels like shifting sand? What do we do when, or if, our faith falters? We fall back on our Experience. When we acknowledge our Experiences, often overlooked because they didn't fit life as we understood it, we can find our faith again. However, this time our faith will be supported by Experience. Now it becomes: I know because I've experienced, rather than I believe because someone told me.

This is powerful! This is where faith becomes stronger. This is where we can now seek guidance to navigate this world while much of what we thought would last forever is beginning to crumble. We can find our strength through faith plus experience. The New paradigm of spirituality will be Faith + Experience. When we add our deep or unexplained experiences, accept them and try to learn from them, we have an opportunity to develop this as our own personal guide. Now we have a roadmap to that new way of being in the world. This new roadmap is simply called, **"The New Message of Love."** While it is simple, it is also profound, complex, and multidimensional. It takes our ideas of diversity to new levels. It challenges our thinking. It provides answers to what was unknown. It brings communication to levels considered only by a few. And it gives the steps to owning the power of Love and allowing it to manifest in your life.

Through The New Message of Love, you go from believing in Jesus and His life and teaching, to being Love incarnate in the world.

Jesus used energy to heal the sick. Is He telling me to do this also? Yes.

He fed the hungry. Does He expect me to have compassion and act? Yes.

Did He accept people as they were, and move them forward on their individual paths? Yes.

Did He expect me to accept rather than to judge? Yes.

When He sought justice, was it for revenge? That would not be consistent, as He forgave His adjudicators. He forgave those who followed their orders to crucify Him. He forgave thieves and welcomed them into eternal life.

He didn't judge to levy punishment; he used His judgment to ascertain where people were operating within their hearts, and then gave them opportunities to expand and raise their vibration to one of Love.

Jesus healed. He healed so people could function out of Love, not anger and hate. He accepted people where they were, but He didn't stop there. He invited them to follow Him.

He gave up His ego in order to be Love incarnate. He knew one couldn't do both. Ego is dependent only on one's personal power. With Love energy, a human becomes transformed and empowered! He didn't promise lives of luxury; He promised lives of fulfillment that come from serving others.

Consider this: If every life has a divine purpose, would all needs be met? If everyone chose to follow his/her purpose, would all necessary roles be filled?

An empowered life is one that assumes power through surrender of the ego, and expresses Love energy. This is what Jesus meant. This is what is expanded upon in "The New Message of Love." It provides a path for the spiritual seeker not only to live by faith, but to expand understanding and become spiritually empowered through carrying Love Energy.

Jesus Was His Name

His name was Jesus
He was a carpenter by trade
A fisher of men by calling
He had an assignment
He was born to show another way
The Way was Love.

His was the greatest Message
Because it joined heaven and earth through Love
He received guidance from beyond
And manifested the Message on earth
His short life changed a world in darkness
He is my Lord and my Brother.

Now the world's gone dark again
Children killing children without remorse
Greed supported by philosophy: end justifies means
Technology moving faster than the culture can contain
Poverty leaving more people behind
Hate being fostered by institutional rage.

The New Message of Love has arrived
Change of heart perhaps slower than change of mind
The New Message of Love faces doubters
But those who are ready, can receive.
Open your heart and focus on Love
Be a light in a world of confusion.

The New World will become empowered
Through opening to "The New Message of Love."
It provides guidance to navigate rapid change
Guidance to communicate mind-to-mind
Guidance of whom to marry, whom to avoid
Guidance for choosing a different way.

Guidance for surrendering to Love
Guidance for opening to channel
Guidance for choosing friends and finding life purpose
Guidance for fulfilling your mission in the world
Guidance for life well-lived and lessons understood
Guidance for returning to Love.

Once again the world is in need.
The light of Love is again being revealed.
Those who are disillusioned can receive
One must become disappointed to become open
One must know pain to open to healing
One must know Love, to return. And so it is again.

Chapter 2

Taking Our Religion to a New Level

'Nothing stays the same." How often have we heard that? However, our response may have been, "My religion doesn't change. Jesus' Teachings don't change." His Teaching doesn't change. That is true. But the interpretation of His Teachings changes as the world changes. We need an interpretation of the Teachings of Jesus that is relevant to the New World.

In the world when Jesus lived:

> There were no cars, buses, trains, planes.
> There were no electronic devices.
> Teaching was done in person and through repeating stories.
> Teaching was an event, not accessible at all times.
> People depended on one another to transmit culture and traditions.
> Wars were contained.
> Family was the central unit.

In the New World:

> Communication across vast expanses is instantaneous.
> People strive for money during all of their working years.
> Success is measured by status and wealth.
> Wars are global.
> The environment, even the planet, could be lost by our decisions.
> Ego needs seem to outweigh all others.
> Trust is being eroded in all of our institutions.

People are confused and react rather than act.
People do not act in an accepting, tolerant, caring manner.
People are being divided and manipulated by outside forces through their media.
The human-centered view of the universe has been found false.
Humans find themselves with an identity problem: In this universe, where do we humans fit?
Humans will need to unite in order to maintain human freedom.
Humans must give up trying to stay unique and separate, to unite and stay alive and free.

The New Testament is as relevant today as it was 2000 years ago, but only if we interpret it for the time in which we are living. The New World is here! Life will never go back to the ways we knew. We will need to adapt in order to survive.

We don't mind change if we initiate it. We want it to be our idea. We want to shape it until it is the way we want it before we share it with others. Others will want to make the changes palatable for themselves. So, we accept change that we initiate.

We do not like change forced upon us. However, that's what is happening. We liked being able to make calls at our convenience, so cell phones gave us that power. However, we are becoming unhealthy by being available to others at all times. We achieved the convenience at the cost of our health.

It's a New World!

Childhood answers to the big questions aren't true.
> What we believed in is often fallible.
>> People whom we trusted fell from grace.
>>> Ideals we lived for seem to be fading from human values.

Truth is mostly perspective, not absolute.
> What was yesterday, is gone.
>> Today will be gone, tomorrow.
>>> People come into our lives only to become distant memories.
>>>> Or they vanish, without a trace.

The New World is the old world, but dramatically different.
> What was predictable, is not.

No longer can we depend on climate stability.

It has been replaced by an ever-changing and often volatile environment.

Mores accepted by various cultures have been infiltrated.
> No longer "pure"; no longer unadulterated: West and East are co-joined.
>> What has replaced the cultural norm is variety.
>>> Races are combined. Languages contain a variety of multi-lingual expressions.

What was accepted as "good" no longer exists in common vocabulary.

Literary works of artistic expression are replaced by the text and video of the moment.

Everything is moving fast. What was new yesterday is already outdated.

Even the "techies" are challenged to keep abreast of the technology du jour.

Yesterday's phone is considered a joke, while movies made during one's lifetime soon seem dated and remote.

Abilities and technologies are expanding.

What we thought of as stationary is charged with energy that flows, moves, or becomes stuck, creating illness.

Origins of illness are becoming more obvious as our demanding lifestyles keep us stuck in unhealthy life patterns.

Old species disappear; new species arrive.

Faster than we can name and categorize them, they appear where the existence of life was thought impossible.

The New World is full of what was believed to be impossible— from the movement of craft to the emerging abilities of humans.

> We can no longer expect the old ways to support new challenges.

We need, **"A New Way for a New Day!"**

Consider your childhood, and that of your parents and grandparents. What changes do you see between them? Children born today will know nothing of what your grandparents experienced and soon will not be familiar with what you experienced. Parenting is constantly adapting. We can't raise our children for the world that is already gone. Even more difficult, we must look forward and raise them for the world in which they will live, but we cannot even imagine!

The New World needs a Message relevant to this time. The world needs, **"The New Message of Love."**

Chapter 3

Inspired by Changes, or Changed by Inspiration?

What motivates you?
What makes you want to be a better person?
What makes you want to make an effort?
What shuts down your desires?

We are unique, yet similar. We each have people, places, and beauty, that inspire us. Sometimes other people say things that make us feel more awake, at ease, hopeful. Others, whose minds are closed to new information can feel as though they are dragging us down. If we are to improve, expand, grow as a person spiritually, we cannot allow those committed only to the past to stop our growth. As humans, we are here to grow. If a child stopped developing, it would have implications for his/her future. It is also true for adults. Growth is something we are designed to do all of our lives. New information and experiences bring in new perspectives.

This is also true of our religion. We are expected to grow. Jesus said, "Follow me", yet He could do miracles outside of human reach (Mark 8:34). Yet that didn't stop Him. He didn't say, "Follow Me a little, or for a short distance." He said, "Follow Me!" Do as I do—heal the sick and broken-hearted; lift up the dead. The miracles He performed became our inspiration and our aspirations. If we are to be like Him, we need to allow ourselves new experiences and information. We need to use our religion as a starting point, not an ending. We need to take all that we have learned and build upon it. That's what He intended.

What are your thoughts and experiences that you have doubted because they didn't fit what you felt you knew to be true?

Society is giving us many occasions to question how something fits into our beliefs. We couldn't fly through the air at great speed in Jesus' time. We couldn't prescribe antibiotics to heal infections, perform CPR when hearts have stopped beating, or see the great art of the Louvre electronically. We didn't limit our discoveries because they didn't fit into the life at the time Jesus was born. We expanded our thinking, made new discoveries, healed the sick and at times saved the dying. And now, we are being asked to expand our view of religion to be relevant to this New World. How will it change? It will need to incorporate what we have learned through experience.

We have reached a tipping point. We can no longer deny the experiences of so many because it is more convenient to do so. The numbers of people having experiences outside the framework we have constructed as reality are staggering! It compels us to open our minds to what is actually occurring. It demands that we see what is actually happening, not simply what we want to believe. And, as we do so, we are being called to expand our religious framework to include these, as yet, unexplained experiences.

What do we say to the dying person who sees family near their bedside? Do we deny their experience, the experience that brings them comfort? Or do we allow this by saying, "Mysterious are the ways of the Lord." When we do the latter, we are opening our thinking to allow for what can't be seen, and yet is; what can't be heard, and yet is.

Many of us can allow for death-bed visions because they are so commonly reported. While science can't confirm them, and has at times attempted to explain them away as oxygen deprivation to the brain, this event is now so commonly experienced that it is accepted by many. Our nurses and physicians, who care for the terminally ill, have witnessed patients during these events and could enlighten us much more. We need only to listen with an open mind.

Some people see things that our paradigm of reality says cannot exist, and yet the experiences persist. Ghosts, apparitions, are a part of our culture, yet if asked, we might have to say that what they see is impossible because within our generally accepted view of reality, ghosts can't exist. Yet they have been reported throughout history.

In 2021, the world was given a much greater challenge to our human definition of reality. Our religions are being challenged now as perhaps never before. Those religions, including Christianity, will have to answer the question, "Can we incorporate what we now have confirmed, that we humans are not alone in the universe?" Can we accept the idea that perhaps humans are not at the center of the universe? If so, what will that mean?

"When a paradigm shifts, everything goes back to zero." A man named Joel Barker made this idea popular in the 1990's. The example often used was that of the famous Swiss watches, known at the time as the gold standard of watches. New companies began making digital watches. With that one change, a move to digital time-keeping, the paradigm shifted back to zero.

Change isn't always so apparent. Often, we can recognize it by looking back. Compare childhoods of different generations, and you will see rapid change, which seemed slow at the time it occurred.

The Pentagon announcement that there are aircraft with capabilities unknown to humans entering our airspace is the challenge of our century. It means everything goes back to zero. That which we believed couldn't be, is. The ramifications of this admission are deep and are already shaking the trust we have always placed in our institutions! It is challenging those institutions that so strongly denied this possibility. What happens to our trust? What happens to society if the institutions we trusted fail as a result of lack of trust? We cannot allow that to happen! Our only way to save our society, and it must happen quickly, is to find ways to incorporate this new information into our current frameworks for religion, education, government, mental healthcare, and more. Our institutions, all that we developed that functioned well, are now challenged as never before to change. Those that change may survive. Those that are unable, will fall away. This is the new reality, and our ability to adapt will determine our future, and the future of our world.

THE NEW REVELATION

"Who Do You Say that I Am?"

When the wind blows, and the newborn cries
When at death's door, and when in pain
When you want to hide, and have no place to go
When all you know has fallen away—
    Who do you say that I am?

When you want to cry; When you're all alone
When the storm's all over, and the damage complete
When the sight of fear is the sight of man—
    Who do you say that I am?

When the river runs dry and the sun parches lips
When all you have known turn their backs to you
When the wind is howling,
Or the seas roar
    Who do you say that I am?

When does life begin? When does it end?
Is it predestined, or completely your choice?
Are plants and animals only for humans, or humans remiss about their import?
When no answers come
    Who do you say that I am?

When death is looming at the hospital door
And the world keeps moving like all is the norm
When life comes, And life goes
    Who do you say that I am?

You Are Love
Christianity Transformed

When you deny me in public, Deny me in schools
When you teach the young there is no recourse
When they take their lives rather than face the emptiness—
    Who do you say that I am?

When there's no place to run,
And no place to hide
When the planet's time is up in a moment of choice
When a single decision determines your course—
    Who do you say that I am?

I Am the one you will return to. I Am abiding peace.
I Am the light in the darkness. I Am the port in the storm.
I Am here when all else fails you.
I Am here at beginnings and ends.
I Am all that is left when nothing else remains.

I Am your Source, to which you'll return
I Am Alpha,
And Omega, too
I will be your only comfort.
I will be there when you awake.

For, I Am always with you, Recognized or unrecognized
I am what you want even when you reject all
I am the light in the darkness that does not rely on the sun.
I am the hope in your heart when there is no reason to hope.

I am the rain that cools,
And distributes over the earth
All the seedlings that grow.
I am the reason, the reason to live
When humanity is only a memory.

For humans deny,
And humans partake
They make mountains of molehills, and molehills of mountains
They seek pleasure all day, and avoid pain at all costs
While remaining oblivious to consequences their choices will drive.

So, don't cry for humanity when it cannot continue
Others are waiting patiently to overtake them
Their freedom lost, their pleasures denied
They failed to listen; they failed to take heed.
But now they Know who I Am.

Chapter 4

It's a New World Requiring an Empowered Faith

"He's got the whole world in His hands."

(Traditional African American spiritual, first published in 1927)

This is known in our hearts to be true. We don't need to explain it if we've lived with these words in our hearts, on our lips, and in our perception of the world. One Creator, God, or Source of all that is. We are created by Him and will return to Him. This is our faith.

Inside that faith are many smaller constructs—differences of thought. We call them Baptists, Catholics, Presbyterians, etc. But all claim one Source that became human to show us how to live. To forgive. To love. To care and care for. We as Christians are united in our main principle. How we break that down into smaller paradigms of religious beliefs and practices differs somewhat, but the essence remains.

Why do we want to limit God, Who is limitless? Why do we want to say that something can't be because we believe it can't be? Doesn't that deny what we also say, "With God, all things are possible"? Yet perhaps we don't believe that, because we can be very black and white in our interpretations.

Some of us believe that "He's got the whole world in His hands" means just that, and is not limited to Christians. When we open our minds to that concept, we can stop warring for religion.

How do you explain "world"? Only world? Or does He have the whole universe in His hands. Or even, Universes?

Why would we limit God to loving Christians? Or only humans? Perhaps we should study why we humans choose to limit our description of God. Love. World. Universe. Does He love it all, without limitations? Can we truly choose to serve a limitless God—a God who loves without limitation? The sinner and the saint? The Christian and all other religions? Those without religion? Those who aren't human?

"Nothing can separate us from the Love of God." (Romans 8: 38-39) The most beautiful and reassuring words of all. Nothing. Nothing outside or inside us. No other being. Not even our own behaviors. We are already loved because we are all a part of Love. Love is God.

What does that mean, "God is Love"? (John 4:8) It doesn't mean that God is like Love. Or God loves. It defined God with only one word! Volumes have been written, but here was only one defining word! God is Love. So simple, yet profound. If we believe it, do we also believe that He wouldn't leave us without direction when so much is changing and we are suddenly in a New World? No. He sent, "A New Message of Love", which does not deny any of our past, but builds upon and expands our understanding.

If we believe God is Love, we believe He is Love for eternity, not just in the most recent 2000 years. "The New Message of Love" expands upon our understanding to make it relevant for our time. It's what a loving God would do. And did. He gave us a Message through a Messenger who has learned to hear beyond our common definition of hearing.

This messenger is not alone. Love has been speaking to those who "have an ear". (Matthew 11:15). For "he who has an ear, let him hear." We can all open to this new way of hearing.

Remember as a child learning about the "still small voice" (1 Kings 19: 11-12)? It's speaking loudly now. Open your heart and mind to hear it. Open to, **"The New Message of Love."**

You Are Love
Christianity Transformed

Chapter 5

Receiving the Invitation

You are invited. What powerful words! Love is inviting us. Will you say, "No"?

Our life is our RSVP. It is our response to the Invitation to Love. What will you say? What will you do?

If God is Love, then the "Invitation to Love" is the invitation to God. What does it mean? It means that we left Love to be born into a world of much chaos and confusion so that we could find our place and help resolve and eliminate that same chaos and confusion. We are here with a myriad of choices and questions. Education? Career? Lifestyle? Partner? Children? Use of leisure time? Use of our energy?

Each of us comes face to face with these and many more choices. The most important choice we make is whether we choose Love (Energy that supports, accepts, guides, clarifies, heals) or Fear (energy of division, confusion, disruption, despair, violence). That choice of energy is the choice we make for this lifetime. What is your choice? Why?

To really understand the Invitation to Love, requires understanding Love. How do we know if we want it if we do not understand what it is?

Love is Energy. It is not human or non-human. It is not the energy that runs our cars or heats our homes. It is an energetic force that moves us forward in a direction if we choose. It is something we have learned to call upon with our multitude of requests. It is our next step to understand Love, or God, as an energetic force that can become part of us—something that we carry. Once we invite and accept that powerful Love energy into our lives, our lives will begin to change. Externally we may appear the same. Internally there is rapid change resulting in a shift in consciousness.

Today, New Age language includes words like shift, consciousness, and awake, and many practices are built around these concepts. This has also given rise to the business of spirituality. For our purposes here, we will make a distinction.

Spirituality is the acceptance of ourselves as spiritual beings inhabiting a materialistic world. In spirituality, which often separates itself from religion, one is free to taste and learn about a wide variety of spiritual practices. From that smorgasbord of meaningful options, one finds those that intrigue and challenge them, and the person adopts the spiritual practices with which he/she feels a resonance.

Thus, the person on this spiritual path is a seeker of truth, of a way to live in harmony with nature. Many businesses have been developed that claim to help the spiritual seeker, or spiritual sojourner. Crystals, different styles of meditation, dietary changes, and even clothing and jewelry to help identify one to others, proliferate. Some have become more refined with many spiritual offerings for purchase. Spirituality, like much of religion, has become big business. Once it becomes business, there are those who have a stake in its success and rewards.

God is free. Love is waiting patiently. Love endures. Love carries. Love divides and separates all that is not of Love. The last statement is a powerful attribute. Love only accepts that which is of Love. The remainder falls away. Once the Christian makes the decision to take the next step and commit to a deeper understanding and expression of Love, life begins to change. It is uplifting, joyful, to make this decision to commit to this deeper level of Christianity. You may begin to notice changes within yourself: less desire to be a part of noisy, busy celebrations or events; more time for internal reflection. Who am I? Where am I going?

Nature may come more into focus as we begin to feel more like a part of nature itself, and to be valued and preserved, rather than benefiting from its destruction. You may feel less like a consumer as your thoughts turn inward. You begin to place more value on time alone or with a few close and accepting friends, and less need for acquisitions. The material world begins to shed its glamour for that which is real. You begin to see yourself as a participant in life where real problems exist needing solutions. You may even feel drawn toward helping find solutions—healthcare or wellness, abuse, justice, the environment, or many other issues needing resolution. You begin to want to serve —to leave the world a better place, and you will feel a tug, perhaps gently at first, to move you in the direction of your spiritual purpose, or how you came to serve in the world. Now you have moved from measuring your success through acquisitions and status, to measuring your effectiveness in helping others. It is a huge shift, and it is life-giving for the person, and all those around him/her.

After accepting the Invitation to Love and making a deeper commitment to Love, challenging issues may occur. Although you may not be aware, you have begun to carry more Love energy. As you meditate, reflect, and grow, your capacity to carry Love energy increases. Some people are very sensitive to energy and can recognize a feeling of Presence. Others see the results. All that is not part of Love will begin to fall away. You may need to heal addictions, forgive those where you would prefer to hold onto anger, or resolve long-held resentments. Others may not be consciously aware of the energy you carry, but react as that energy begins to disconnect relationships.

Relationships at this stage must be supportive of your spiritual growth to be able to continue. Nothing must be allowed that will take you off your path. You now require the out-of-sight assistance you are becoming more aware of, but you also will separate from those people, values, lifestyles, and jobs, that undermine your new commitment. You are like a seed that falls upon the ground, vulnerable to the wind, rain, and temperature, as well as those who would use it for sustenance. So, the New Christian must be aware that support for this new commitment must be the priority. At times, partnerships, even marriages, have been severed when the partner is unwilling or unable to support the New Christian. Thus, one of the most painful and confusing parts of accepting Love, is allowing that which cannot go with you to fall away.

There are many benefits to accepting the Invitation to Love that cannot be measured by the traditional measurements in society and business. The benefits are partly intrinsic to the New Christian, but it is also the world that benefits.

Consider coming into contact with others unknown to us. Love energy helps us determine with whom to become friends or do business, and whom to avoid. The Love Energy you now carry recognizes only that which is meant for you, and you may note a sense of discomfort that, if bias is not present, will tell you that this person or situation is not right for you. Thus, Love Energy guides, protects, and makes you aware of what is meant for you, and what is to be avoided.

Relationships are powerful determinants of one's success. If one person is devoted to a direction, it will cause disharmony if the partner is against or unsupportive of that direction. In this new definition of a primary relationship, the relationship needs to allow each person to express as they are designed to express while being mutually supportive. The glamour of romantic love may excite, but frequently does not lead to the kind of relationship that supports this deeper level of commitment resulting from saying, "Yes!" to the Invitation to Love.

You Are Love
Christianity Transformed

Surrender

Dear Jesus,
I want to trust in Your power and grace;
I want to look in Your loving face;
I want to know that You really care;
But, tell me, Jesus, are You really there?

Some say You are, but is it so?
Is it just a mirage, an afterglow?
Do You really care when things go awry
And the only question we have is, "Why?"

There's a space in my soul that is empty now;
It needs something big to fill it, somehow.
If You're really there and You really care—
Then I'm ready to take the dare.

I'm ready to chance that You'll do as You said—
Come into my life, give it hope instead
Of the doubt and fear that fill it now.
Come into my life, if You really know how.

Come into my life—I'll take the chance
That there'll be a change, some kind of advance;
That somehow in a way that I don't understand,
You'll fill my heart; You'll take my hand.

You Are Love
Christianity Transformed

Yes, I took that chance a long time ago.
I don't understand, but I love You so.
You gave me new life, filled me with joy,
And I feel like a kid with a brand-new toy.

You lifted and loved, gave me new worth;
You gave me new hope, a joyous rebirth.
I'll praise You, love You, give You my life;
Surrender it all, till there's no more strife.

You Are Love
Christianity Transformed

Chapter 6

Taking the Journey

Congratulations! You have made the commitment and are ready to begin the journey. It is marvelous. It is difficult. It is full of ups and downs, joy and pain, fear and reassurance. It is life—magnified, and with purpose. No longer will you need to doubt, regret, and use the glitter of the world to escape. Your life now has definition, and is demanding. There is little time for self-doubt. There is much to do.

To the outside world you will appear quiet, perhaps even withdrawn. Your party-loving friends may begin to pressure you for time. You may begin to need less time for social events, and more time to get to know this new life, this new you, better. You are not withdrawing, or becoming a recluse; you are discovering the richness of your internal life and appreciating its many dimensions.

Journey to Love was given through a Messenger to prepare you for the world as a New Christian with a deepened commitment. It is important to mark the date of your commitment, and celebrate it annually with a deepening recommitment. You will find that rather than limit your life to a set of acceptable behaviors, the annual recommitment will serve to take you to deeper levels of experience and understanding. As you do the daily Steps of Journey to Love, you will begin to unlock parts of yourself long hidden even to you. You may become more aware of what is honest, and what is deceptive. You will learn to determine if words and actions are congruent, and who is not living truthfully. The efforts toward deceit by society will become more clear. Your values will become more clear to you.

You may also develop your gifts, long held latent within you. You may not only see, but "see through" deception. You may learn to hear beyond the words being expressed to the unspoken message. Your intuition may become at first awakened, and then honed. This is extremely important, for intuition guides us regarding what is safe, and what needs to be avoided.

You will become more aware of another's energy. This will guide you as to whom to trust, and who must be avoided.

As your Profound Intuition continues to develop through the Steps in Journey to Love, your gifts may begin to develop. For some people, the development of a gift they carry is essential to be able to perform the individual unique purpose we each are designed to contribute.

Once you have made the decision to accept the Invitation to Love, made a commitment and celebrated it, the next step is to do each of the Steps in Journey to Love. While we each take the same Steps in Journey to Love, the experiences provided will be unique to each person. In life we each have the same lessons: loss, grief, joy, birth, death, fear, hope, relationship, lack of relationship, sickness, and health.

Each life has these, but the actual experience is unique to the person. The same is true with doing the Steps. If you start a Journey to Love group to do these Steps together, the actual experiences you each have may differ.

You are encouraged to start your own Journey to Love group. It will be more like a support group as you are beginning together. If this has a deeper meaning for you after you have completed the entire process, you can contact New World Empowerment Center regarding becoming a New World Empowerment Minister. This is not a requirement for anyone, but available if this is where your spiritual path should lead.

You Are Love
Christianity Transformed

Chapter 7

From Pain to Gain

Humans evolve spiritually through lessons. These lessons include opportunities for courage, faith, honesty, and integrity. From the joy of new birth, to the grief of loss. Each lesson is given until the lesson is learned.

One example where humans often face a challenge within the lessons, is in relationships. If one keeps choosing a significant other who is abusive, the couple may separate only for one to choose another abusive partner until the lesson to empower oneself is learned. This is the beginning of self-love and the end of what may have been a family history of abuse.

When one is in the throes of illness and/or disability, one may feel worthless. When jobs are lost as a result, the person may feel no longer worthy, and therefore unlovable. This lesson presents the opportunity for self-love to emerge, and for the person to choose a different and often more rewarding job or path. When the disability is limiting, the person may begin to re-invent himself/herself, this time taking time to do personal inventories of skills and preferences in order to move into work more in line with his/her spiritual purpose.

The discovery of one's spiritual purpose is often borne out of disappointment and disillusionment. Marriage is forever — they say. Build a career, not a job — they say. Find your one true love — they say. Choose the dream of marriage and family — they say. Those are the ideals with which many were raised. When the marriage cannot continue; when you are laid off or fired from a job; when the politics of the organization don't allow upward mobility; when one's body can no longer perform the previous work, there is often a crisis. This crisis of faith that everything would work out the way it was "supposed to" can be a dark and lonely period. However, even in the midst of this crisis, especially if others intervene and support, rapid spiritual growth can occur.

It has been said that earth is a school and we have come to learn. The spiritual sojourner, the Christian, seeks to depend upon faith to help recover, and bring change to life. At this time of great growth, one may have experiences that help to recover faith. Experiences are what help us know something. Experiences strengthen faith. Faith is belief and trust in what we have been told. Experience is knowing because we have experienced. Faith plus Experience is the basis of The New Christianity.

Love is something we are taught, and also something we experience. Poets have long written about the attributes of love. Romance novels give us unrealistic views of passionate love. Romantic love is connected to sexual gratification. Romantic love is often the spark that sends a couple reeling in their new-found mutual experiences and preferences, only to be stopped by some differences that cannot be reconciled. And so the romantic partners leave one another to find different romantic partners. This can be exhilarating for a time, but eventually leads to loneliness and disillusionment.

When a partnership is discovered through mutual concerns and desire to make better lives or opportunities for others, the couple may find togetherness in pursuit of mutual goals. Here the relationship may develop a foundation that can last. Relationships that serve spiritual purpose are often discovered through mutual activity rather than ideation of the other's virtues, only to be disappointed at the inevitable lack of perfection.

When the Invitation to Love is accepted in one's heart, the events of life may continue but be interpreted differently. The person who might not have met a romantic ideal may be viewed within his/her service, sacrifice, or love of family. Thus the criteria of romance may blind one to the ideals of a relationship that allows both to follow their unique spiritual purpose.

Love is God. God is Love. Often, we are most aware of Love in times of great stress and anxiety. When a beloved family member is critically ill, one may find Love in the midst of loneliness. It is also at this time that we may be more likely to call upon, and depend upon, Love. Regardless of the outcome, we will have come through the experience of Love. It is often at this time that we realize that Love now needs to be the driving force in our lives, and not merely where we turn from time to time.

Sometimes we can see Love at work in another's pain. Those fighting with addiction, who have surrendered their lives to Love, often improve and go on to live empowered lives filled with Love energy. Sadly, those who didn't choose Love, often continue their desperate lives of addiction.

Those who had especially painful childhoods, sometimes turned to Love out of their desperation. They may still have endured a long struggle to overcome, but they did it with strength provided by Love.

We become empowered by choosing Love. That kind of empowerment is spiritual empowerment, and it can grow to be powerful. The New Christian is one who not only believes, but has experienced this power, often in difficult times. It is then necessary to nurture and grow this new power, to protect it from those who would destroy it, and allow it to be guided from Beyond.

Many of us do not want to give up what we think of as freedom. We think that if we surrender our lives to God, or Love, we will lose control. We may act like children; demanding life be done our way. The Guidance we receive when we ask will take us in the direction already prepared for us. To gain this empowerment and allow it to grow, we need to nurture it not only through prayer, but also meditation. This is where many Christians balk, fearing that they will become vulnerable to the devil. God is great. We have heard that from childhood. When we ask for protection from any unseen, we are protected. Meditation is opening to Love, allowing Love Energy to lead, and choosing to follow Love where it takes us.

Prayer is asking for our needs, and sometimes wants, to be met. Meditation is opening to receive. How can we expect to follow Guidance if we cannot allow time to listen? Allow several minutes of silence at the end of your prayers, and you have entered into meditation. It's that simple, yet profound. Your meditation can be where you are most comfortable. It can be in church; it can be in nature. You may be sitting quietly, or walking. What is important is to be in silence. You may be in a group with a leader of meditation; you may join an online meditation such as the International Peace Meditation where people from around the world join in anytime during a 24-hour period. Love is timeless, and as you do this, you join in consciousness with others. It is beautiful to contemplate all those beautiful souls, joining across boundaries of location, religion, race. This joining of consciousness toward peace empowers the individual and increases Love energy in the world.

The world is full of pain. Love Energy is the antidote. When we surrender to Love, open to all its manifestations, we become Love in the world, and bring light into darkness through the Love Energy that we carry. Love Energy is. We do not need to act as though we carry it. It precedes us so that others notice that there is "something" about us, but are not yet able to define it.

As we grow in our ability to carry Love Energy, others will move forward to join us, pull away, or may react negatively. So, the New Christian, the Empowered Christian, must always be aware of other's reactions.

While this doesn't demand that we act pretentiously, it may result in natural changes in our behavior. We may avoid loud, crowded areas, preferring to be able to focus internally. We may lose our desire for the glitter of the world as our lives become filled with meaningful activities and relationships. The Invitation to Love invites each person, every person, to a life rich with Experiences that deepen faith. We no longer believe only because we've been told; we believe because we have Experienced. When life-challenging events come into our lives, we now have a stronger foundation through Love.

The Journey to Love will not be easy, as life is not easy. However, the difference may be that the New Christian seeks to learn the lesson from the painful experience. How we interpret events while and after they occur will be more life affirming, and less likely to leave us bitter and lost. Sometimes these painful events become catalysts for life choices. For example, advocating for those with an illness is often the result of that illness having affected our lives.

The Journey to Love is the most important and relevant journey you can choose. It is a journey that continues after the

Steps given have been completed. It becomes a way of living. It becomes the way of life. The New Christian has surrendered to Love, committed to and taken the Journey to Love, and carries Love Energy in all he/she does. It is not enough to act lovingly. We are now called to be spiritually empowered. This new empowerment, with guidance from out-of-sight, is how we will navigate the challenges of the New World.

Joy in the Pain

We'd shape our destiny; we'd draw the plan;
We'd take control. And so we began
To make true our dreams; but now they're a sham.
There's no joy in the pain, somehow.

We thought we knew how, right from the start
To hold high our daydreams and follow our heart.
But free-will, reality, fate played a part.
Can there be joy in pain, somehow?

We fight God; we curse Him; we give Him our back.
We blame Him; misuse Him; then others attack
For their faith seems just pious when all hope we lack.
There's no joy in our pain, somehow.

That course is destruction; its victims all fall
To unfathomable depths for self-pity to maul.
But just at that point if on God we will call
There'll be joy in that pain, somehow.

He picks us up when from cold we are numb;
When moaning and crying have left us dumb.
When we turn our hearts upward and in let Him come
Soon there's joy in our pain, somehow.

We give God that daydream forever to hold;
Let go and just trust that our life He will mold —
Knowing that through pain we have entered His fold.
Now there's joy in that pain, somehow.

You Are Love
Christianity Transformed

Sometimes that pain is still ours to endure.
Now only comfort and release hold allure.
But God takes our spirit; our emotions find cure.
Now there's joy in the pain, somehow.

Thank you, Father, for the joy that is mine.
Thank you for the pain that made me Thine.
Thank you for your Presence; make me Your sign.
Oh there's joy in my pain with You.

Chapter 8

The New Christian

The New Christian is empowered by The New Message of Love and Love Energy. These New Christians are brave because they took the Bible and expanded upon it by including the power of Love Energy gained through The New Message of Love. The Message invites, and shares the Steps to becoming spiritually empowered. Capacity to carry energy increases with time, attention, prayer, and meditation.

Love Energy heals. It goes into the deepest darkest places, even beyond our memory, and releases stuck energy. It moves the person to forgiveness of others, but especially of oneself. Who can be a New Christian and hate God? Hating oneself, the vessel for Love Energy, demonstrates a lack of understanding. We are not alone with God, or Love, out there in the vast somewhere. We are carrying Love Energy into the world to first become healed, and to heal others.

What does it mean to be healed? It is not the same as being cured. We can be healed of anger, lack of forgiveness, and resentment, and that makes a positive contribution to our physical health, but it does not guarantee a healed body. Sometimes one can experience healing, yet that complete physical healing may be only able to occur beyond the physical body.

The New Message of Love speaks of many lifetimes where the soul is given opportunities to learn, grow, and contribute to the betterment of all. Lessons learned from previous lives carry into the next life. Lessons not learned will be presented again in different ways until the lesson is learned.

It is like a beautiful staircase of vibrations. As each lesson is learned, one ascends farther up the staircase, acquiring more Love Energy. Love Energy is a high vibration, and each Step raises one's vibration. Those whom we encounter react first to our energetic vibration, and secondly to our words and actions.

If you enjoy being with animals, you can see how they respond to vibrations. Animals react to low-vibrations with caution, even threatening if they feel threatened. Yet they often react positively to the person carrying Love energy as they feel that higher vibration and seek it out. You may notice how dogs will react uncharacteristically to a new person, either negatively or positively. Animals rely on their instincts for survival. Humans have lost much of their innate intelligence because of social behaviors that attempt to cover truth. When the words someone is saying seem right, but the feelings you are getting do not, be cautious. This is your built-in protection from those who would hurt you. Use it carefully and wisely. Recognize when you want to believe the words, but your gut is reacting. This is your warning to be alert and aware.

As you progress farther into the New World with its coming challenges, it is Love Energy that will be there guiding, pulling you toward some, and away from others. Do not confuse these feelings with your desire for a certain outcome. Do not let your fear overwhelm you when it "feels right." Listen internally. Ask yourself, "What are my instincts saying about this person or situation?

Another important aspect of being an empowered Christian is developing beyond what we normally think of as seeing, hearing, and feeling. There is so much to be developed over time. As you meditate regularly, you may find that you are able to see energy that surrounds a person. Some people see auras. Some see colors that may indicate state of wellness. Sometimes people use this expanded gift to enhance their professions. Those in healthcare sometimes add energy healing to their skills. Some musicians hear internally. Some writers can tune in to an energy where they can receive thoughts, even messages. Some people learn to channel this way of receiving information at will. This form of hearing is internal and does not require an eardrum. It is given directly, thought to thought.

Many Christians cringe at something new, fearing it is satan or devil-worship. If you are an empowered Christian, you will be guided to explore. Jesus said, "Follow me." He meant, "Do as I do." So when we use Love Energy to heal, we are following Him. When we open to that "still small voice," we can hear beyond what our physical ears can hear.

Consider Jesus in the garden. He wept. He knew what He had to do. He asked to have the cup (death) taken from Him (Luke 22:42), but when He was guided otherwise, He accepted. He received information. He heard beyond physical hearing. We can learn to do as He did, as He told us to do.

Jesus' teachings have always been open to interpretation. What do you think He meant? Did He say that we should build palaces and empires to bow down and worship Him? He said, "Follow Me." He told His Disciples to become "fishers of men" (Matthew 4:19). We need to find those in pain, hungry, injured, sick, lost, and grieving, and help them become whole again. He healed the sick, and raised the dead physically and emotionally. Can we, then, do less?

When we minimize Jesus by becoming judgmental and exclusive, we are not living as He did. When we cannot separate our respect for human law, from what He has commanded — that we "love one another as I have loved you" (John 15:12), we run into difficulty. When we live as an Empowered Christian, we become open to others different from ourselves. We are not to ask who we are to love; we are simply to love.

Love will define us. Our increased energy as we attain higher vibrations will define us. But just as important, Love Energy will guide our decision-making if we allow. It is not easy doing the Steps in Journey to Love, but it is more than worth the effort.

Christians already have a foundation in the Bible. The New Message of Love prepares us to receive guidance to navigate the New World. The Empowered Christian has acquired Love Energy by doing the daily course of study called "Journey to Love."

While is it important to read the Bible and Invitation to Love for understanding, it is even more important to do the daily experiential exercises in Journey to Love. This is a critical step in becoming an Empowered Christian. Empowered Christians transform Christianity.

The New Message of Love breathes new life and hope into us. It is further evidence that God, Love, does not leave us comfortless (John 14:18). The New Message of Love helps us navigate the New World in which we now live.

Christianity Transformed now becomes for each of us, "A New Way for a New Day!"

Chapter 9

Healed! Empowered!

What does it mean to be healed? To be empowered? These two words are used frequently in many settings. However, it is necessary to define them here so that the New Christian may understand healing and empowerment within this context.

Healing begins on the emotional level. Much that causes humans physical pain has emotional origins. Pain sometimes manifests early, such as stress stomach aches in children when they are afraid or angry. However, as the child develops, they often learn how to mask these feelings in order to hide them from others. Pain is held inside, only to reappear in health issues at a later time.

Today many realize that there is a mind and body connection, and look for opportunities to treat the patient on both the emotional and physical levels. As the patient progresses in self-understanding, the source of much pain may be revealed. Childhood abuse, whether or not intentional, by children or adults, may rise to one's conscious memories. Even long-forgotten memories may surface to be reviewed, and then viewed from multiple perspectives. Forgiving oneself for "mistakes" is also an essential part of healing. Often what is recognized is that these were common human mistakes and not deserving the misery we have inflicted upon ourselves as punishment.

Once healing of the emotions begins to occur, it is often then that pain lessens. While it may never be completely erased, the power of that memory loses its impact, and healing of the body begins.

Once healing begins, empowerment can also take root. Empowerment begins when we make room for power through the process of healing. As this negative energy is released, it leaves space for new energy. If one is grateful for the relief caused by emotional release, the energy is positive and opens one to more positive energy.

A human is "empowered" when filled with positive universal energy called Love Energy. This energy multiplies one's power and effectiveness and increases empathy. Love heals. It reaches into the darkest places of human emotions and causes them to unravel. As they unravel, they are no longer a hard block, but have become porous. Once porous, they begin to dissolve in intensity. This dissolution of negative energy and replacement by positive energy allows for true healing to occur.

Sometimes people seek the services of a Healer. A Healer is one who has gone through a healing process, and after reflection and the creation of positive intention, is able to magnify healing energy, causing it to transfer to the other. When this intense energy is received, it moves the blocks within the human energy system. It then progressively causes the dissolution of each block, allowing positive energy and creativity to flow.

A New Christian, who recognizes and studies The New Message of Love, and seeks healing through prayer and meditation, begins dissolving old blocks, healing past traumas, and taking on Love Energy. Sometimes this occurs in the moment. More often, it is a process.

Sometimes the physical damage is too extensive to repair, but the traumatic memories, which created the tension and blocks, lose their power. The person opens to the Love Energy, and begins to share it with others. This is a powerful, positive impact although the impact is seldom visible to the one carrying this Love Energy.

As you go through the Steps in Journey to Love, you will begin to heal internally and to carry Love Energy. Love Energy is what empowers! This energy can sometimes be witnessed through the reactions of others. Some will unconsciously want and seek this energy. They will come forward. You may note this in new people, or people you know with new and positive reactions to you. They will feel an affinity toward you that they do not understand.

Some will not want to be near that Love Energy as it clashes with energy they carry or may be drawn to. They may pull away, fail to return calls, or be unavailable to be together.

A more dramatic response may come from some who strike out at the energy you carry, without understanding. They may develop a rationale for their behavior and blame you for what they feel was an injustice done to them.

The New Christian, who has strengthened his/her faith by incorporating experience, still has much to learn. Spiritual power increases effectiveness, and will create reactions. This power must always be enhanced, protected, and guided through meditation. Therefore, meditation, surrendering, healing, and carrying spiritual power are the essential new parts of becoming an Empowered Christian in the New World!

Acceptance

Tell me, Blessed Jesus,
    When you walked upon this earth,
Did your friends accept your efforts,
    Who once marveled at your birth?
Or did they ever laugh and scorn,
    Make you their fav'rite joke
While your Father's will you strived to do
    To carry each one's yoke?

Did you ever tire of your mission here?
    Wish the nightmare'd go away?
Wish you could be like other men—
    Put in a normal day?
Did you like being a rebel?
    Did you know that you were born
To live and die a humble man
    With only a crown of thorn?

Did you have feelings like I do?
    Did they ever get in your way
Of bringing to fruition
    God's plan for you that day?
You seem to me so brave and strong,
    Were you ever scared like me?
Did you ever cry or tremble,
    Laugh or sigh where men could see?

You Are Love
Christianity Transformed

I'm so glad that you were human
        As well as being divine.
You make my life more relevant,
        I want to be your sign
And yet I feel so weak and scared
        of judgements that I hear;
It's not the heathen, Lord,
        It is some Christians that I fear.

I want to share myself with them,
        Imperfect though I be,
But I find you more accepting
        Than anyone I see.
Help me to remember
        As I share with other men
That you gave your life that I might find
        God as my closest friend.

If He can accept me,
        With all my doubts and fear,
Then only if I let them
        Can others hurt me here.

You Are Love
Christianity Transformed

Chapter 10

Ready to Lead Change

Once one has read **Invitation to Love** and has taken one year to do the essential daily Steps in **Journey to Love**, one may begin to feel more loving, caring, open-minded and intuitive. The Steps are never complete, as it now is one's daily charge to meditate, open to more healing and Love Energy, and share with others. Moriah shared her process in **The Healing Journey** as it shows that life, itself, is the healing journey. As long as one is alive in the body, this power can grow, expand, and begin to help heal the world.

The world is depleted of Love energy. It is a dark time in human history. Each day there are mass murders, and individual murders of bodies and spirits. As the level of human consciousness diminishes, acts of violence increase! Therefore, the antidote to the lowered human consciousness is for healed, empowered people to raise the level of consciousness within themselves, which then begins to raise the level of human consciousness elsewhere.

It may at times seem futile or trite to try alone to raise human consciousness to Love. It is never futile or trite! However, it is even more powerful to do it with others on similar journeys. Jesus said, "When two or more are gathered together in my name, there I am also" (Matthew 18:20). In other words, the power of Love multiplies. Love energy expands. Consciousness expands. The combination of human spirits engaging, carrying, and disseminating Love is powerful!

Sometimes you may see quotes or memes telling you that if you want to change the world, you must begin by changing yourself. As you open daily to more Love Energy, you become more powerful in a positive way. As you join with others on this Journey to Love, you will greatly increase the power of each, and of all. In other words, both the individuals and the group become more powerful. This begins to raise the vibrations toward Love in other places.

It is important to remember that Love does not judge. It is not for empowered Christians to compare themselves with others. This is where many within Christianity have failed. Using self-righteousness to criticize or punish others is not acceptable. True empowerment is the loss of one's ego in the pursuit of Love. It is not for the New Christian to flaunt power, but to share the power of Love Energy.

Some will feel called to leadership. This has many pitfalls if one gets off the spiritual path. In order to become a Leader in the Human Empowerment movement, one must first make a spiritual commitment to Love, or God, and then practice this commitment daily. Taking time for daily meditation, occasional spiritual retreats, and annual re-commitments will help to keep you on the spiritual path. It is essential to remember that the Leader must first model the behavior desired in others. Therefore, it is essential to surround oneself with the relationships that support spiritual work. Inappropriate relationships pull many off their spiritual paths, regardless of the deep desire felt for following it. Therefore, the first and one of the most painful steps, is to evaluate one's relationships to determine if they support this new spiritual commitment.

Once the commitment is truly made, one's spiritual growth is deeply empowered and one becomes a powerful force for Love.

You Are Love
Christianity Transformed

Chapter 11

Be the Change!

As you study the Invitation to Love, you are made aware of its beauty and also its challenges. You recognize that the New World cannot be adequately served without the acceptance and exploration of a newer vision for Christianity.

As a Christian, you already had faith as your foundation. It may have already helped you through painful experiences, such as loss. It may have helped you survive relationships where love was not returned. It may have already helped you to overcome an addiction or bad health habit. It may have improved some of your relationships. It may have made you more accepting of others who do not think or believe as you. It probably had other powerful effects on you. This love is non-judgmental, non-competitive, and allows for a far greater expansion of your innate gifts. Your compassion will increase. You will desire to serve Love and make a positive difference in the world.

By now, much of what you felt was important may seem unnecessary or self-indulgent. You may begin to look at using your remaining life to help others. A need for wealth and status may change: how can I use my wealth and status to help others? You may find yourself returning to dreams in your past: being an artist, musician, teacher. Your dreams may have been shelved in order to become a responsible contributing adult. What were they? Would reigniting and re-imagining them bring you happiness?

Do you ever feel a calling to be more? Do more? Make a difference rather than earn more money, degrees, status?

Now you are opening to possibilities. As you open, meditate upon how you are meant to be used in service to others. Do you feel a stirring causing disruption in your plans? What is that feeling? What does it mean to you? Are you empowered enough to believe you deserve to consider it? To consider life-changes or changes in priorities?

Be Love in the world! At this dark and troubled time in human history, be a light in that darkness. Fill yourself with Love energy. Allow that Love energy to guide you. Ask, "What do You want me to do? When the answer comes to you several times, is consistent, and feels like Love, explore it. If it feels right, you are now learning to follow Love's guidance.

Human ego is always clamoring to be heard. Meditation helps us to silence the ego, its wants and fears, and hear the true guidance as intended. This challenge, of wants or fears, will always recur, and it is up to the New Christian to uphold his/her commitment, meditate, practice the Steps, have spiritual retreats away from the daily demands, and recommit. The recipe may be simple, but the practice just listed is essential. Those who lead from ego are often dangerous and not to be followed.

Go! The world is waiting for you. Join with other like-minded people, whether near or far. Technology has taken away the geographic divide. Do Journey to Love with others. Consider becoming spiritually ordained.

True ordination may be celebrated together in ceremony, but truly comes to the heart that has been prepared to receive it. Moriah's spiritual ordination was powerful and is celebrated through the Messages she received and shared.

Spiritual commitment will allow Love to lead. Spiritual Ordination will make you a Leader.

If you spread Love Energy in the world, you will help to raise human consciousness toward Peace. If you become spiritually ordained, you will become an empowered Leader.

All true empowerment is about opening one's heart and requesting healing, accepting the Invitation to Love, doing the daily Steps in Journey to Love, reflecting upon your healing journey as you read The Healing Journey, and daily overcoming the human ego by opening to and carrying Love energy.

Those who claim empowerment without Love energy are frauds, and dangerous. Many have already led humanity away from Love to violence, fear, and hate. It is now time for a new way. It is time for a new day. It is time for A New Way for a New Day! It is time for The New Christianity!

He did not leave us comfortless

> We are loved
> We are invited
> We are protected
> We are guided
> We are empowered by Love Energy.

Transition

"The Word of God is once again made manifest among us."

The Teachers of Love

You Are Love: Christianity Transformed
is preparation for living in the New World.

Love Energy—Spiritual Energy that enhances one's innate abilities, including understanding, intuition, protection, and capacity to care.

Spiritually Empowered—One who has surrendered to God or Love or Source, and has accepted the responsibility to carry spiritual energy called Love Energy.

New World—A time of rapid evolutionary changes including developing technologies, climate change, shifting allegiances, loss of trust in institutions, intrusions into our air space, new illnesses, pandemics, mutations, spiritual gifts, new forms of communication and transportation, and expanding consciousness.

New World Empowerment Center—A spiritual center for all, providing leadership for a rapidly changing world through the revelation of The New Message of Love, given to Humanity through the channel, Moriah.

Christianity Transformed—an expanded interpretation of the life of Jesus Christ as it relates to the New World. The New Christianity includes:

> Faith + Experience
> Interpretation of Jesus Christ relevant to today and to the future
> Love Energy

New World Definitions

Capacity—the level of spiritual evolution needed to accept new information.

Channeling—the means by which information passes between universes, or the seen and unseen.

Communication—all forms of traditional communication with the addition of energy communication and telepathy.

Experience—a unique experience that is considered impossible within our current paradigm of reality, and may include seeing, hearing, knowing, and sensing beyond the known capabilities of our physical senses.

Experiencer—one who has one or more unexplained experiences.

God, Allah, Source—name given to the Highest Energetic form that has evolved.

Healer—one who channels Love Energy.

Healing—all forms of conventional Eastern and Western medicine with an increased focus on energy direction, control, and enhancement.

Higher Self—that aspect of the human spirit that receives information, processes information for the highest good, and emanates energy which is transforming.

Intuition—inexplicable knowing that exceeds current conventional thinking.

Love—word used for God, Allah, Source, Universe, or highest energetic form. New World Library—the established name for the channeled works of Moriah.

New World Library—the established name for the channeled works of Moriah

Oppression—the dulling and overtaking of the human spirit's right to express. The opposite of Spiritual Empowerment.

Paradigm—the way in which we interpret.

Religion—a path taught as a way to limited spiritual evolution and fulfillment.

Self—the picture one has of oneself that changes as one evolves spiritually.

Spiritual Empowerment—the ability to access the Higher Self for decision-making and guidance, while also emanating Love energy.

Spiritual Paradigm of Christianity—a reinterpretation of Jesus for the New World.

Spirituality—a path one follows to learn and evolve that leads eventually to spiritual empowerment and fulfillment.

Telepathy—mind to mind communication.

Transportation—includes all forms of transport in addition to ability to move without traditional physical mechanisms.

Unity—the joining of those carrying Love Energy.

Will—the determination of the spirit to express.

The New Message of Love is a Preparation for Humans to join with others who are not human.

I. **Invitation to Love** invites you to join.

II. **Journey to Love** provides the Steps for becoming Spiritually Empowered.

III. **The Healing Journey** provides a perspective of life as the healing journey.

Assurance

"I will not leave you comfortless . . . I will come to you."

(John 14:18)

Jesus incarnated as the Son of God, and brother of all. He promised that the Holy Spirit (Energy) would remain with us always. The Holy Spirit, an aspect of God, is what guides, protects, and goes before us. Thus, Energy goes before us, is all around us, and is available to us. Through surrender of our human ego, we increasingly open ourselves to greater capacity to carry Love Energy, which is God. Thus, when we carry Love Energy, we are Love in the world.

> The New Testament Trinity: God, Jesus, Holy Spirit.
> The New Message of Love Trinity: Love, Intuition, and Peace.

All six are aspects of Source, from which we have come, and to which we will return.

> **Love** (God) is an Energy that invites, unites, and fills one to capacity. Once we surrender to Love and begin our spiritual journey, we begin to emanate Love in the world.

> **Intuition** is a profound sense of knowing.

> **Peace** is the presence of Love Energy that fills one's internal longing.

Spiritual Empowerment is carrying Love Energy, accessing it for guidance, and propelling it into the world for healing of all that is not in alignment with Love.

"Be ye not conformed to this world, but be ye transformed!"

(Romans 12:2)

The person who is spiritually empowered is in the world, but not of it. You are spiritually empowered when:

1. You open your mind to an interpretation of the life of Jesus Christ relevant to this New World;

2. You recognize and accept your unexplained experiences, incorporate them into your worldview, and expand your concept of spirituality;

3. You surrender to Love, with intention and commitment to develop the capacity to carry Love Energy.

Faith + Experience + a Reinterpretation of the life of Jesus + Spiritual Empowerment = Christianity Transformed.

You Are Love
Christianity Transformed

Welcome to

The New Message of Love

The New Message of Love was recorded as received with minimal editing. It appears here as received, in the voices of the Angels, in three volumes:

> **Book I. Invitation to Love** invites us to join in concert with those in the flesh and beyond who are leading during this evolutionary change.
>
> **Book II. Journey to Love** is a curriculum that will guide you to develop the necessary skills, perception, understanding, and power to survive and lead.
>
> **Book III. The Healing Journey** provides a view of life as it goes through the stages of healing to true unity or oneness with the Creator, referred to here as Love.

The New Message of Love is given in order to prepare Humanity for the New World in which Humanity is but one of many races in the greater universe. New communication skills, new methods of discernment, and the divine universal energy of Love, will be your guide and protection. The Teachers of Love are high-vibration Beings, also called Angels. The following is their message to Humanity as received by Moriah (Sue Kidd Shipe). The New Message of Love provides the context for what is occurring:

Humans long ago covered instinctual responses with politically acceptable behavior. By learning to deny our gut responses, we also lost some of our self-protection. That is why those who study human behavior in order to manipulate us, such as con men, are often successful.

Energy precedes intent. Intent precedes action. Too often by the time we identify another's intent, it is already too late to protect ourselves. Therefore, by learning to recognize the energy that surrounds and is in a person, we can better protect ourselves from negative intent.

Imagine you are in a group of people. Even within a small group, note which person feels inviting, who feels cold or disengaged, and who feels repelling. What is repelling you? If not words, actions, tone of voice, or body language, then what? Is it, perhaps, the energy that person carries? Note how you feel with each person, even if you do not engage them. When you leave the group, note your energetic experience with each person. Did it draw you closer? Feel like boundaries were protecting? Or repel you? Keep in mind that you, too, carry energy and others are responding to that energy.

Love energy, or spiritual energy, is very powerful. As the person on a spiritual path deepens his or her commitment, the energy becomes stronger. As a Step on the path is taken, the energy increases. As your energy increases, others may have stronger responses toward you. Some will be drawn closer, some will pull away, and some may even strike out. Keep in mind that when a person strikes out verbally or physically, with no apparent reason to justify such an action, it is likely the energy you carry that evokes this response. The perpetrator is not even aware of why he or she does not like you. They may create a story of how bad you are to justify their actions to themselves.

Consider Jesus the Christ. He was full of Love energy. He carried so much Love energy that people were drawn to him for healing and the Message. Yet those without loving hearts or carrying Love energy, questioned his motives and saw Him as a disruptive force. They killed Him because of the Love He carried that inspired His words and flowed energy to heal the sick. **They had to see Him as evil to justify their own feelings and actions.**

Those brave people throughout history, who carried great love and wisdom, were not accepted. They were seen as a threat because love is often seen as a disruptive message. They had followers, and appeared anarchistic to those who feared losing power. Many were destroyed because others could not tolerate them, their Love energy, and their words. Yet, their Message of Love lived on.

And now it is time for another Message. The **New Message of Love** is a gift from high spiritual Beings, called Guides or Angels. This is their gift to Humanity, given through Moriah.

A Message from Moriah

Why me? This question still floats into my consciousness, as the work I am given to do is so profound. How is it that I, once an isolated girl from the center of a little-known state in the United States, felt the weight of a calling from a very early age? How is it that with no formal theological training, I have been given a Message to share with Humanity? If it's a Cinderella story, then it has deep implications for you—for each person: your life has even more meaning for others than it does for you. Life is more than surviving, even thriving. Your life is your message to your family and to the world of who you are and what you value.

Moriah is the spiritual name given to Sue Kidd Shipe. Angelic Beings called The Teachers of Love channeled The New Message of Love through Moriah, during a period of over 20 years. It is presented here with the addition of "You Are Love: Christianity Transformed" for those who are looking for a more relevant interpretation of the New Testament as it relates to this time of rapid evolutionary change called the New World. You Are Love: Christianity Transformed is Christianity's next step.

Moriah receives Messages through telepathy, or mind-to-mind communication. It is a way of hearing without sound. Thoughts are transmitted, and "heard" mentally. The Steps in Journey to Love are given to provide each person a course of study to develop his/her own special gifts. It is not simply a novelty; these are skills that may be required for a specific spiritual purpose and for one's own protection. Seeing, feeling, hearing, knowing, and sensing are abilities that can be developed far beyond our physical capabilities. Each Step will take you deeper into that new journey of experience.

It takes faith to say yes. It takes faith to surrender one's ego, and follow. That same faith, when combined with new understandings and newly recognized experiences, is the foundation for The New Christianity.

My journey was given direction by my spiritual ordination. I was home alone. There were no clergy or sacraments. The vision of an Angel pouring gold light upon my head and the words "You are ordained" were my Spiritual Ordination. It was a profound and lasting experience. I knew. I did each life step as I understood it. I learned to meditate by simply showing up, intending to meditate. I received the information, recorded it, and now I am sharing it. I wear a ring that is my commitment to my path. I opened my heart to receive; and now I'm opening it to you.

This is sacred writing. While perhaps no other topic has received more attention, it is not just another book about love. It is a Sacred Text given as the next step for Humanity. It is given to help us survive the challenges we have not yet imagined.

I share it with an open heart. It may make your current ministry more alive and relevant. It may give your life more meaning. It may provide help through you to those who are suffering spiritually, physically, or mentally. It may help you discover your true purpose in life. It is yours to study, share, love, follow, depend upon. It is up to you how deeply you desire more spirituality in your life. It is your decision to Be Love in the World.

If you're like me, you may find that the God-huge hole in your heart can only be filled by Love.

The New Message of Love
I. Invitation to Love

Book I.

Invitation to Love

Introduction

Invitation to Love was received by Moriah in 1991. It was given over a period of approximately five months, one chapter at a sitting. Now, 25 years later, it is being made public. Its message is relevant to our time as we increasingly move forward as a global community through communication and technology, exponentially expanding our knowledge of our planet and our universe, continuously challenging notions of "reality" and our scientific paradigm–and literally, reaching for the stars. We are increasing our awareness of ourselves internally and externally as we progress.

At such an important juncture in human evolution, while many people still view human life as the only life in the Universe, an intervention called "The New Message of Love" is offering to us a broader and higher perspective of reality. We are given a vision of our evolving earth and the challenges the human race will face. We are helped to understand that while we struggle with accepting human diversity, we will be given a greater challenge as we expand into a universal community. What we learn here may amaze and challenge us, but we are also given a way to adapt to this change. Invitation to Love is one part of a broader message, The New Message of Love, being given to us through Moriah by the highest level of spiritual entities known as Angels, or Teachers. Their messages will continue to be received and added to the writings that form the basis for New World Empowerment Ministries. More information can be found at www.newworldempowerment.org.

If at first your mind is rejecting of this new information, simply read, and then let it be. Everywhere our paradigms are shifting. What was once believed impossible is now possible. What was once accepted as the norm is now outdated, even obsolete.

Reflect on the change you have witnessed during your lifetime, and you may find little today that is even remotely reminiscent of the lives of your parents and grandparents.

The next great step in spiritual evolution will be based less on faith in another's story, and more on personal experience. This is not to challenge, but to build upon existing religious and spiritual beliefs. We are opening to new experience, and as we do, our lives become more relevant. Here we are given a way to achieve and maintain stability while our world shifts. Old ways of thinking, living, believing, moving about, and even viewing ourselves within this ever-expanding universe are changing. What we believe, the institutions we've trusted, and our view of life purpose, are all shifting as well. We search for the meaning of our existence and wonder why we are here.

These age-old questions find new meaning in spiritual experience if we are open to it. However, we cannot yet imagine the beauty, life, purpose, and fulfillment this contains.

You have come here for more. What you long for is here. What you need is here. What the human race needs for its successful evolution is here. Open your heart to receive the Invitation to Love.

Invitation to Love is given here as it was received, with minimal editing in order to maintain its authenticity.

Invitation to Love

A Gift from the Teachers of Love to Humanity

The Invitation

Devotion to God is the highest order of Love. Love has many levels and manifestations. Your people use love when they mean fantasy of romance, acceptance, caring. Yet these levels of love do not generally require surrender and sacrifice.

Higher levels of Love may require more of one's self to be given. In romance, one is seeking self-satisfaction and self-aggrandizement. In other words, one's ego is generally boosted as one is placed upon a pedestal and admired, and one might find this quite satisfying until life experiences create a reality that does not allow for this to continue. Caring may be made manifest in many ways and is most essential to the proper nourishment of all people. Caring is the emotional environment that promotes growth. Yet, Love, as it is a manifestation of God, may require that all that one has be given.

When one loves in this manner, one seeks the highest good. One chooses actions based upon understanding from one's higher self. This view is from a different perspective than the perspective that celebrates romance. In other words, relationship based upon the highest good emanating from one's higher self will be that which is manifest by higher purpose.

The New Message of Love
I. Invitation to Love

Love that devotes all of self to God is the highest order of love, yet it must be emanating from one's higher self. In other words, it is sometimes seen in your world that there are those who proclaim to love God, to seek followers, yet their actions are for their own aggrandizement. When one gives oneself to God, there are no accolades. There is only fulfillment. That fulfillment is unity with the Godhead. This unity with the Godhead is what joins all within the universe. Thus, all joining is becoming one with God.

The spiral of Love moves through many levels. One must go through many incarnations to reach the level of devotion to God. Thus, one must not look out upon the world and judge the world, but recognize that all are joining. All are in process. All are returning. One must not feel sad for another who cannot join, but see that they are on a path of learning so that they may be able to contribute. Many incarnations must be provided for this learning to occur, and one must also be able to see beyond the glitter of the world.

One comes to devotion to God through disillusionment. Therefore, as long as one is somewhat satisfied by the world's offerings, one will not come into the desire to devote one's life in service to one's higher purpose, to God. Therefore, one can only come to God through disillusionment. It is when one has tried to find fulfillment in the many areas available within your world that one becomes resigned or disillusioned. One may remain in disillusionment or may use this disillusionment as a catalyst to propel them into a newer life. This new life is a life devoted to one's calling in the world. Therefore, it is only through the pain of disillusionment that one may be reclaimed.

All who join are being reclaimed, as all were once joined. Incarnations are the separation of one from all others. It is this decision to incarnate, to learn and contribute, that creates separation, and it is the decision to accept the Invitation to Love that causes one to return. Therefore, in each incarnation one is given the opportunity to join. Most will go through many incarnations, and upon joining, will move forward into the next level. A few will be given the choice to return upon having accomplished joining. They will bring a Message incarnate. The Message will be of God.

Those who return incarnate will need support by those preparing to join, and they will move together to the next level upon completion of their assignment. Therefore, the chain is unbroken as those from Beyond give the Message to those who choose to return, who offer the Invitation to all others to join. Those who become incarnate out of a decision to return as Messengers must carry a heavy responsibility alone. Yet they are never truly alone. The memory of Home must be reclaimed as one loses all memory upon entering the earth-plane. Your people are without memory of Home. They must reclaim their memory. They must join in order to return. Therefore, this Message is the Invitation to Love, to join, and to return.

You are invited. None may be excluded. All are encouraged to join. Let your life be given in devotion to God that God might work through you and thus bless and reclaim your world. This is most essential as your world continues in its evolution, as this evolution will be the bringing together of beings of many worlds. This is already occurring. You must turn away from the glitter of the world and make a true choice, the choice to fulfill your purpose and calling in the world that you might move forward and that the Universe might become One. Thus, all are joining. All are returning.

All will eventually be One.

The New Message of Love
I. Invitation to Love

The New Message of Love
I. Invitation to Love

The Word of God is made manifest among you. It is the reclamation of intuition that will bring all to peace and love. It is God's will that your planet reclaim intuition that all might return Home. Honor those who are reclaiming throughout your Universe. It is to be desired that all shall follow.

Do not allow those desires of your personal self to draw you away, as they are only vapors that disappear in light of day. They sparkle, they glitter, they draw you like an oasis draws a thirsty man, yet only that which is of God shall be reclaimed. Therefore, it is your people, your community, that is to be the leadership of your planet. They will assist in bringing forth peace and love. It is only when your desire nature is true that others will recognize your devotion and follow. Therefore, it is not to first draw upon others, it is to first purify yourselves. Take this word to all who will truly commit their lives to their spiritual purpose. It is in the commitment and bringing forth one's purpose that others are drawn.

One must move forward alone, willingly acknowledging that God is all one needs. It is when one can let go of oneself, that one draws what is needed to them. Therefore, let your lives be unburdened. Let your souls be purified. Let your desire be for God. Speak to no one of your purpose, for your purpose will speak to all.

Do not allow that which would be unrequited take you away from all that is of eternity. Speak of love and peace. Live love and peace, that love and peace may speak to the world. It is God's plan that all should follow; therefore, move forward that others may see God's peace and love and be reclaimed.

The New Message of Love
I. Invitation to Love

The Love of God is deeper, stronger, more enduring, and completely fulfilling. It will be the manna for your soul. Therefore, from this date forward, let nothing take you away from that for which you have been anointed.

Speak only of God's love, God's peace, that they may abide with you and through you. Allow all who would to follow and bring forth all that is of God. Your light must now begin to truly shine, that the world might see and yield.

God is Love. God is Peace. God is Intuition. God is Trinity. One experiences God in the realms of intuition, love and peace. Let the Trinity be the redemption of your planet.

The New Message of Love
I. Invitation to Love

The New Message of Love
I. Invitation to Love

Love is the fulfillment of the heart's greatest desire. It is the reclaiming of the world to God. Love is the vehicle that transports one to that place where all longing is fulfilled. Love provides the answers to all of life's questions. It takes away doubt. It heals wounds. It guides the lost. It promotes the bringing of your planet to its ultimate conclusion. The ultimate conclusion is the returning of all to God. Therefore, it is the bringing forth of Love that will provide your planet the necessary means to return Home.

You are beginning that total Love experience. It is the desire to give all of oneself to God. It is the desire to hold back nothing. It is magnetic. It is that which the more one experiences, the more one desires to give. Therefore, once one begins to accept Love, one surrenders personal power and gains the power of the Godseed. As you move forward in Love, as you truly allow yourselves to become channels of Love, you will lose yourselves more and more completely until all has been released.

As you move forward to make this eternal commitment, you are letting go of all that you have known to gain all that you truly long for. The world does not define that longing and seeks to fill it with those things that are only temporary. There is much sadness, much pain, much suffering within your planet. This is created by looking in the wrong places to find one's true fulfillment. It is by stepping forward that one can truly move into the Light and allow all else to fall away that one might become one with One. It is as you move into the Light that you return Home. You accept Home and bring Home into your world, but you are already Home.

As you move forward in the world, your experiences will change because you have changed within yourself. You will begin to see differently, to hear differently, to experience the world as a place where healing can come through you. Therefore, the healing power of Love will go out into the world and touch all pain and suffering.

The presence of those who are in this Light, who are channels of Love, is both disruptive and healing. Therefore, one must be prepared to witness what is occurring to realize that the presence of Love is at work, and to allow Love to do what It must to allow change to occur.

Love is power. It enters and does not leave. It ignites without consuming. It propels one so that one no longer wishes to control in the way one once did. It is by allowing yourself to release control, to become unburdened, that you become channels for Love. Let your prayers be that you might relinquish all. Let nothing keep you from the Love of God. Be willing to step forward alone, that others might join you, for it is in the willingness to be alone that one is never alone. One gains when one gives up. One moves forward when one stops running, when one allows Love to imbue their lives and move them in Love's direction.

The New Message of Love
I. Invitation to Love

Love knows nothing but Love. It cannot recognize what it does not already know. Therefore, Its presence will be most challenging. When one is a channel for Love, one must be able to move about, knowing that disturbances will always occur. One will make others feel uneasy, doubt themselves, fear; and the fear will sometimes cause others to strike out. Therefore, one must be most cautious as the power of their presence can create difficulties, they might not otherwise be aware of. It is important that as you move forward, you be aware of others' reactions to you. You must be most discerning for your own protection, aware that another's response may be harsh or one of aggression. Yet Love will provide the healing that is required. It will provide the acknowledgement of all that needs to change. It will not allow things to remain as they are.

As you move forward into this light, you will become purified. You will find yourselves being transformed so that you cannot return to your former self. The commitment you are about to make is your decision to follow God. God is Love. God is Peace. God is Intuition. God is Trinity. The world is in need of these mighty words so that it might return. Therefore, move forward and allow nothing to take you away from fulfilling your purpose.

Meditate on Love, that Love might fill you, might consume you, might propel you, might move eternally through you, to bless your world.

Be at peace and all else will follow.

The New Message of Love
I. Invitation to Love

Love is the devotion of one's heart to its Source. Love brings together all who would join. It will be the redemption of the Universe.

Love asks not what can be done for It, but what one can do. It is when one loves that one allows oneself to be magnetically drawn to the Source of all being.

Love enhances all that is of its own. It saves the world from its own destruction. It is when those who are drawn join together that Love moves forward in the world. It is the moving forward that unifies, that allows the Universe to become One.

Love melds separateness into one eternal being. It draws together positive force and repels all negative energy. That is why one must begin with self-love. When one loves oneself, one can be the positive energy that draws, that joins, that creates, that magnifies all that has preceded.

As the joining occurs, it is like a ball of energy. The ball becomes larger, brighter, more magnetic. It draws more toward it. That is why, as you develop self-love, as you join in small groups, these similar groups come together and begin that positive energy field that will draw all back to the Source.

Love is joining. It is expressed in relationship. That is why it is most essential that when you join, you join another positive force. It is when these two forces come together, they create more than what was once separate. They are more than double. Therefore, the sum is far greater than the parts.

You want peace in your world, yet peace comes from joining. Peace is the product of that which is joined. When you join with others, you will create peace in that part of your world.

Therefore, it is important to continue these joinings. These joinings are happening at both levels of your universe. They are happening among people, and they will happen in the greater universe. It is as these different levels come together; all are drawn upon.

When you are a channel for Love and Peace, you are God's magnet. You are drawn to join with that which is positive. This positive energy is at the level of the higher self, yet it is the personal self that can be most destructive. Therefore, though one sees through the eye of Love, and sees another's higher self, one must be most discerning that one does not join with the negativity of the personal self. One therefore must have double vision. One must be able to see the beauty of the higher self, yet one must be able to look without judgment, without preference, without fear, at the manifestation of the personal self.

One can only join when the energy from the personal self is positive. Therefore, it is important to send out your energy to attract all that are positive. It is important to send Love and Peace to those who are not yet ready to join. They will join in time, so do not become distraught about them, as it is not yet their time for joining. It is this positive energy that comes through those who are channels for Peace and Love that must attract other positive energy.

Love joins positive energy into a magnificent, positive force. This positive force continues to grow. As it multiplies, it brings Peace in the hearts of those who are redeemed. Therefore, Love and Peace are truly One. As these mighty works are taken into the world, they will each manifest. They will each grow. They will join and bring together all who will respond.

The Love of God captures, sanctifies, all that It joins. It purifies all that is Its own. Once purified, Love gives of Itself and becomes a dynamic force. Its magnetic field becomes stronger as it grows.

Love does not know negativity. That is why all negativity, all that is not aligned with Love, falls away. This is the process of purification. This purification makes one acceptable as the offering, as the light, as the energy of God.

This energy goes through one and into the world without one's effort. One's effort is directed at maintaining that purity, of that single-mindedness that one belongs only to God. Therefore, the purification process is never complete until one is Home, yet as one draws closer to Home, one's desire becomes greater, one has less resistance, and one knows that Home is what one desires most of all.

Therefore, let your prayers be that you may be sanctified, that you may be purified, that you may release all that would separate you from this holiness, and that you might forever be channels of Love and Peace.

The world is not accepting. The world fights that which it does not understand. The world is like a frightened child. It becomes threatened and retaliates at all that does not appear to belong. Therefore, those who become channels of Peace and Love must be discerning. They must always be aware of the power that emanates from them. This is not their power. This is not personal power. This is the power of God.

The channel for Love and Peace cannot control the power, cannot control the response to the power. They can only control their own behavior. They must be with Intuition in making all choices. They must know with whom to share, and with whom they may not.

The New Message of Love
I. Invitation to Love

The Love of God satisfies, fulfills, and brings one to everlasting peace. One finds peace as one allows oneself to be purified.

Let your lives be pure, be open, be receptive. Be channels for Love and Peace, that the world might be redeemed, that all might return to the Source.

The New Message of Love
I. Invitation to Love

The New Message of Love
I. Invitation to Love

The New Message of Love
I. Invitation to Love

Love is the heart's full bloom. It is what the heart most longs for. As one grows in the understanding of love, one feels like a bud that is opening, that is bringing forth its full fragrance into the world. As the bud grows and develops, it is at first very tight. It is not open. Yet the internal growth that is continuing within its outer shell causes it to at some point burst that outer shell. As it opens, it begins to emit its fragrance. It begins to receive stimuli from the rest of the world. Its petals are exposed. It is more at the mercy of the elements. It needs to be able to receive the light, the water, the nutrients of the soil, in order to continue to grow.

You are like the bud. As you develop your training, knowing that you have desire for love, but are not yet exposed, you become like a bud that grows until it finally bursts its outer shell. During that internal growth period, you are at first most disillusioned. You are tiny, you are compact; the gentle love of the world cannot reach you through your shell. It is only as this disillusionment becomes most intense that you begin to filter in ideas, information, relationships that cause you to begin to grow. As these new ideas begin to take hold, you are growing and growing until this outer shell bursts and you are ready for experience. Once you have reached the stage where you can begin to experience the love of God, and to recognize it as experience, you are also most vulnerable to strong winds, to heavy rain, to snow and hail, to drought, to lack of nutrients, to lack of those things that would allow you to continue to grow.

Therefore, like the bud which has just burst, you must surround yourself with those who will support your growth, who will love you unconditionally. You must let go of those things in your life that no longer nurture your new discoveries, that will not allow you to move forward. It is this unburdening that is a somewhat difficult part of growth. Yet as those petals reach forward into the sun, they cannot return to the casing that once covered them, that once kept them from all they could experience. That is why, as you move forward into spiritual experience, you cannot return to the bud you once were. The bud is tight. It is closed. It is impenetrable. It is so small, so hard, so closed that it will wither if not nourished. The person on the spiritual path is like the bud growing until it bursts, and then having experience with those things that it needs to be nurtured, and to develop further. If it does not receive these nutrients, it cannot go forward.

Every decision in life now becomes most important in supporting the one who is opening to God's love. Every decision must be made in light of its impact on one's spiritual experience. The relationships one develops, the vibrations one experiences, the interpretation one gives, are all most important. As one begins to have spiritual experience, one begins simultaneously to encounter many who will deny the experience. They are most afraid of disillusionment. They will choose to interpret these events in light of their own experience. If they are of important position in society, they are given much credibility. Their words are given much weight. Therefore, while the criticism of some does not necessarily contain a threat to the one on the spiritual path, the writings and thoughts expressed by those held in high esteem can pose a severe threat because of their personal power. Therefore one must realize on the spiritual path, one is responsible for one's own interpretation of events.

It is important to be surrounded by those who have interpretations of events that are realistic, that are honest, yet are seeking higher purpose. It is important that they be discerning, yet that they not have their vision limited by current and old ways of thinking. They must be open, they must be able to realize that it is not possible to interpret these events within your current systems. Your science, mathematics, literature cannot explain that which the person on the spiritual path may experience. Therefore it is important to be able to trust one's intuition, as one must consult one's intuition to interpret the experience.

Spiritual work is like being on the cutting edge, as one is open to new realms of understanding. One does not have a current system in place for one to recognize and understand these events. One's only way of filtering and testing these events is with their own intuition. That is why the person on the spiritual path must be most grounded, and must have spiritual understanding and intuition available to assist their interpretation. Without this, people have had most amazing experiences, but have been left afraid and unable to function effectively in the world.

As you move forward in the experience of God's love, it is important to have a foundation for interpreting experience. Therefore, one must cultivate one's intuition in conjunction with experience to be able to sustain this work. Without the cultivation of intuition, one is like a flower that opens to the elements and is pushed back. It is as if intuition were the firm roots under the soil that cannot be seen, that cannot be felt, yet it is the recipient of the nutrients. It selects the nutrients needed and filters these nutrients into ways that they will be used for the support and growth of the new blossom.

As you develop in God's love, your roots must become most strong. They must be well developed under the soil. They must provide the support system for all new growth and experience. Therefore, your ability to assimilate spiritual experience is directly proportional to your ability to be with intuition.

One on a spiritual path must have deep desire. It is like the desire of the blossom for the sun. Your desire for your Source is like the desire of the blossom to face the sun. If it is denied sun, it will not flourish. It will turn in the direction of the sun. It will stretch its stems, its leaves, in that direction also. It will reach, as nothing else can nourish it. If it is denied the sun altogether, it will die.

If you, as one on a spiritual path, are denied your Source, you will not be able to continue. Therefore you must seek, you must desire, you must make time for receiving the nourishment of God. The blossom must spend time daily in the presence of the sun. You must also spend time daily in the presence of your Source to receive the nutrients you need for continued growth. This is why, at any time, you can lose your opportunity to blossom by being denied your Source and by failing to cultivate intuition within.

As you move into this light of Source, like the blossom that leans toward the sun, you will become most beautiful. You are full of promise like the bud, yet you must be able to develop, to lose your shell, and to desire and seek the nutrients you need in order for the promise to be fulfilled. The promise of the bud is that it will fully blossom, become totally open, and give all of its fragrance to the world. You are designed to open, to give all that has been prepared, into the world.

The New Message of Love
I. Invitation to Love

The New Message of Love
I. Invitation to Love

Love is the final review of the opportunities and choices one receives within one's life span. Love is the final opportunity to become that for which one has been designed. It is when one enters into the earth life that one comes prepared to reveal one's purpose to the world. One's purpose has already been determined. This purpose was agreed upon before one came into the earth-plane. It was arranged to meet the requirements of acquiring the next step in one's own evolution. This evolutionary process is ongoing until one returns to one's Source. It is like a magnificent ladder. Each rung represents a step of accomplishment, the acquisition of learning and the demonstration of that learning in the form of contribution. The world is a place much in need of the contribution of each person. There will be peace when each person contributes that which he has brought with him into the world to contribute. Therefore, as each discovers his purpose, as each contributes that purpose to the world, the world is coming closer to that state of oneness called peace.

Peace is the unity of all that has been created. It is more than the absence of war. It is more than the receiving all of one's desires for personal acquisition. It is the complete unification of all that God has created. Therefore, peace begins internally with one's own self-love, and continues to encompass all others until there is total acceptance. The world is to be loved unconditionally in its current state. One cannot wait to love. One must accept all that is and contribute to the current state without judgment. When one accepts oneself, another, one's community, the world as it is, one is filled with internal peace and love. That peace and love flows into the world as positive energy. Thus, when one becomes accepting, one simultaneously becomes a channel for peace and love. This will be the redemption of the world.

The New Message of Love
I. Invitation to Love

When all are accepting, when all become channels for peace and love, there will be peace among you. This acceptance is the lack of judgment that says, "I love you just as you are. I see your strengths. I see your weaknesses. Together they combine to bring about this most beautiful person with much to contribute to the world."

One cannot wait until one is without weakness to contribute to the world, as one at this level will always have weakness. Therefore one must accept oneself as one is, realizing that one is uniquely designed to bring forth a purpose. That purpose is not dependent on all strengths. It is dependent upon the combination of specific strengths and specific weaknesses. It is essential as you become more aware that you are designed to bring forth contribution into the world, that you begin to look at your life. You have acquired much that is not relevant to what you are discovering is your purpose.

Your purpose will require your focus. Before you discover your purpose, the whole world is your option. You can pick and choose from a vast array, yet as you become aware of your purpose, your must pare down and choose only those things which are in alignment with your purpose. When one is paring down one's life to prepare for contribution, one may feel pain at giving up those things one has found to be important.

Yet it is this unburdening that brings one into the light and prepares one to be a full contributor. Thus by giving up, one gains all that one is designed to fulfill. One has the opportunity to take that next step on one's evolutionary ladder.

Love is the final redemption of the heart's longing for its Source. At this stage one has conscious awareness of one's desire for God. Through lifetimes one has learned the lessons to be learned, and has assimilated that which was to have been part of that preparation. One has agreed upon the task to be given to the world in order to take another step in the evolution toward Home. As one fulfills the contribution at that step, one takes a giant step in one's own evolution. Yet one does much of this outside the conscious awareness that one is moving Home. One knows that one must, as one feels a sense of urgency, yet it is truly the desire for God that brings one to the fulfillment through contribution.

As one progresses into the fulfillment of one's purpose, one finds increased desire to bring that purpose to fruition. One will feel rejuvenated, full of desire, with more life flowing through them. This life they will experience as energy, as enthusiasm, and it will provide the strength to make the decisions that are in alignment with their own purpose. Therefore, moving up this ladder, moving toward the fulfillment of one's purpose, is like being pulled by a giant magnet. As one moves toward the source of that energy, one is drawn most strongly, and that attraction becomes stronger as one moves forward.

Like the tiny bud that has cracked the outer casing, the petals flow forth freely and quickly. They can no longer be contained. They have desire to give of their beauty, of their essence, to the world. Thus one who is fulfilling one's purpose, who has made commitment to that purpose, suddenly finds their lives quickly unfolding and their desire increasing. They find that they have a need to experience the giving of that which they have brought with them. The stage of preparation, which is love, is like the bud which contains much growth. The next stage, which is that of breaking the casing, cannot occur until the preparation is complete. The preparation may appear incomplete, inadequate, as one nears the fulfillment of one's purpose, as one feels oneself being thrust upon the world. Yet the casing cannot break until the preparation is complete. The flower, when it opens, is a total and complete flower. It is small, yet its petals will peel away independently of one another, causing the appearance of rapid growth.

As your casing is broken, and as you emerge on your spiritual path, you cannot return to the bud. The petals can never close together in the manner that they once were. Your life can never go backward; it must go forward. You must bring your gifts to the world, that your gifts can contribute toward the peace of God.

Love is the magnet that draws you to full contribution and the achievement of peace. Love is the redemption of the planet. It is the magnet that pulls all to the Source of all that has been created. It is this love, this acceptance, that promotes the growth of each individual. Therefore, when one is a channel for Love and Peace, one must be aware that one must be most accepting in order that each person will experience what it means to be loved unconditionally, that their own intuition will be activated.

It is the activation of this intuition that brings them to purpose. Therefore, Love is the link between the activation of intuition, and the peace of God. Love is the catalyst. Love is the activator. Love is not always gentle. Love can be most painful as it brings one toward the truth so that they might move forward with their own purpose. Love is both soothing and disruptive. It soothes, in that it stills the unexplained longing within the heart by moving it forward. Yet it is often preceded by disruption, which causes one to move. Therefore, think not that Love is for soothing one into a state of complacency. It is, rather, the motivator of one toward the fulfillment of one's purpose.

As one begins to bring one's purpose into the world, one becomes a channel for love. This Love can be most disruptive. As one is fulfilling one's purpose, one must always be discerning so that one takes care of oneself. Others will react, yet it is not a reaction to one's personality, it is a reaction to the God presence within. Therefore, the one who is on the spiritual path, and who has broken that casing and begun to allow one's purpose to be fulfilled, becomes a most disruptive element in the presence of others. One must be loving and accepting, yet one must be most aware and shield oneself. There are those who will be able to participate, who will be able to encounter the truth of acknowledgement that their lives are for a deeper purpose. Those who make this decision in the presence of Love will move forward to contribute their gifts.

Most will not be able to accept and understand the truth, will move away to protect themselves, and if threatened, will strike out. Therefore, the person on the spiritual path must be most non-threatening, must be assertive and able to move forward, yet must not create those situations for direct confrontation that would endanger one. One must be most with Intuition, so that one can discern the level of confrontation of truth that one may bring forth. Therefore, Love is most disruptive as it brings one into position of encountering the truth within them. This is most painful for many, and one must be ready to love and support another as they deal with this truth. That is why honesty is so important when one is on a spiritual path. One must be able to speak the truth, realizing it will cause disruption and possible hurt and anger.

The magnetic force of God pulls all in the direction of returning to the Source. It is that which will bring peace individually, and to the world. It is a contribution of gifts that gives one internal peace and makes one a channel for Peace and Love. Therefore, as one moves forward on the spiritual path, like the flower that is in blossom, one must give all of oneself in the journey. The journey is most glorious and brings people forward to the heart's desire. Ask that God propel you forward on your journey, filling you with lifeforce that keeps your path straight and brings you to the peace that surpasses understanding.

The New Message of Love
I. Invitation to Love

Love is the basis for all relationship. It is the tie that binds one to another. Love brings forward in each that which is best. It promotes the growth of the other. It provides the strength and the support to allow for the other's total growth. Therefore, when one is in true relationship with another one feels most supported; one feels most bound; one desires to give forth love and support. When these qualities are not present in relationship, the relationship is not truly supported by love.

There are many other connections that can bring about relationship, but they are not of the kind that foster true relationship in the world. As one looks at one's relationships, one needs to have criteria for deciding if those relationships support their growth as an individual, toward becoming all that they are to become to fulfill their purpose in the world. One must look to these criteria to determine whether one is supporting oneself in a way that will allow them to bring their lives to this point of fruition.

In determining whether those relationships are supportive, one is not to be judgmental, one is not to desire to hurt another, yet one must be most objective. One must look at the relationship and ask, "Does this relationship support that which I am to do in the world?" If one's life is dedicated to a higher purpose, to a sense of mission, one will have much energy and enthusiasm toward bringing forth that goal into the world. When one is moving toward that goal, one's being is filled with joy, with excitement, with enthusiasm. When one allows other things to clutter that path, one becomes most frustrated and loses sight of one's goal if the clutter is not cleared away. Therefore, one must look as to whether one is feeling enthusiastic, one is feeling excited, one is feeling joyful, to determine if one is clearly focused on their goal.

If one does not have these feelings, one should look inward and say, "What are those things, those relationships that are not in support of my reaching this goal?" This is not to look at others and say, "You are the reason I cannot reach my goal. You are hindering me." But rather, "The things that I need to support me are not present here, and I must find that support in order to be able to fulfill my purpose."

When one has a sense of purpose, one also has a sense of the enormity of this purpose. It is not for oneself that one gives, but one gives that the world might be enriched. Therefore this giving is essential for the betterment of the world. It is not that one should feel better than, inflated over, others, but that one is contributing that which they have the capability to contribute so that the world might be a better place for all to experience and grow. Therefore, as one looks at one's relationships, one must question first what it is one needs. "Do I feel supported? Do I feel that this person with whom I am in relationship truly understands what it is that I am doing, that I must do, and would be able to contribute toward that goal?"

It is not enough that another does not hinder us; it is that the goal can be supported mutually. That is, that both can contribute toward the same goal. This must be a mutual goal in which the two people have different roles to play. One will often be the one who is in the world. This person encounters the people with whom they must participate in order to bring this goal to accomplishment. The other is a more supportive role, going into the world as indicated. Their purpose is often to be the emotional support, the one who takes care of the details, the one who organizes, and the one who soothes the other when the world is not accepting. Both roles are equally important, yet one is more highly visible.

As we look at our relationships we must determine if those relationships indeed support what we believe to be our goal or higher purpose in life. Lack of resistance alone is not enough to say one is being supported, as the fact that another merely does not interfere is not true support. When one looks at relationships, however, and sees interference, one knows that one must relinquish that relationship as that relationship will take them away from the goal and the sense of fulfillment in their lives. If one is a teacher, loves one's students, and desires to contribute to their highest good, one is enthusiastic about this position and needs to be with another who is supportive of that goal. If one is not being supported, one must ask honestly for that support. One must ask the other if they are capable of giving that support. The other must make that determination. Then one must also look at those things that are inhibiting, and ask the other to release or stop those things. If the other cannot accept this, cannot move forward with this new challenge, they must be released.

The second level, that of not being interfered with, must also be challenged to go forward. If that relationship does not provide interference, yet does not give the complete support one needs, one must ask the other: "These are the things that I feel I need in relationship. I would like to have them from you. Are you capable of giving them to me? Do you also desire to meet this goal?" If after much discussion and desire to reach a mutual conclusion, one finds that this relationship is not capable of working toward a mutual goal, one must also relinquish this relationship, as one who is in pursuit of a life's goal must not be interfered with and must receive support. Therefore, one must look at one's relationships to determine whether they are truly supportive.

The New Message of Love
I. Invitation to Love

When one is seeking true relationship, and is not encumbered by a current relationship, one is more free to make choices, to make decisions. This is a most critical point, as the ability to continue toward that life's goal can only be accomplished when one is in right relationship. Therefore, one must be most cautious. One must allow one's self to pursue this relationship only to a point, and if it is not moving in a mutual direction, one must release it. That is why it is most important not to engage in sexual relationship until both have made the commitment to mutual goals. If that relationship is consummated in sexual relationship prior to commitment to mutual goals, there will be much pain at the time that one realizes one must release this relationship, as sexual relationship is most bonding. It is important when finding one's life-mate, that one determine that both are pursuing the same goal or goals before one engages in sexual fulfillment, as this bond will cause much pain and confusion.

If one has restrained oneself, and allowed the separation at the time that it is apparent that one must release the other, there will be more a sense of relief than a sense of pain and confusion. One will then be free to say that we looked to see if we had mutual goals, we realize we do not, and therefore we must part. I will continue to think of you fondly, yet I must go forward and find the true relationship I need to fulfill my purpose.

Thus we can see that love is the mutual pursuit of one's purpose. Choose that person to be in right relationship, so that one is supported toward the fulfillment of one's purpose. When the purpose is mutual, both are supported. It is not that one is supported, but it is a mutual support system. Often one is aware of one's purpose, and the other person is not. As they come into relationship and the purpose is discussed, it will, if the person is ready, ring true. If the person is not ready to move forward to meeting their purpose, there will be resistance and fear, and the person will emotionally protect oneself. This will cause the relationship to become stagnant on that level, though it may proceed on other levels. It may proceed in sexual desire, it may proceed in enjoyment of fun, but it will not be able to proceed at the level of higher purpose.

There are many who share similar goals. These goals are not truly defined. Therefore it is not that there is only one person with whom one can be in true relationship. It is that as those move together who have a common goal, this goal will define itself further into a more distinct higher purpose. Therefore, if one has a sense that one needs to help bring love into the world, one will seek another who desires to bring love into the world. Yet it will be the details of how this is to be accomplished that will become refined as they move together. If one is a teacher and one is a doctor, and both feel they want to serve, it is this common purpose of loving and giving that will cause them to support one another's purpose. There are those who have a highly refined sense of purpose. Their purpose is more specific and is already known to them. They will need to be with one who can be most devoted to that specific purpose. Therefore, there is even more selectivity needed, yet it is the pursuit of mutual goals that is the criteria for relationship.

The media would have one believe that the basis for relationship is sexual attraction, attraction to the physical, and a desire to experience the excitement of what is in the world. Therefore both are always receiving, and both are looking to the other to receive what it is they need. In right relationship, the attraction goes beyond the physical to the attraction of common purpose and the acceptance of one another as they truly are. There may even need to be more time spent finding those things that one can enjoy for fun as the sense of purpose is quickly established. One who loves and chooses to bring forth the fulfillment of specific goals in their life must look to all of their relationships. None of these relationships should be allowed to provide clutter. When one looks at one's relationships, they must determine: "Can I ask for a change within this relationship so that I can continue with what I need to do, or must I allow this relationship to be released?"

One must spend time encountering each relationship and deciding whether it can be pursued or it must be released. One can probe, one can ask questions, one can invite, but at some point one must make a decision. Those people who have made great contributions have done so with the support needed. There are many who had much they could contribute to the world, yet were not able to due to attachments to relationships that were not supportive. Much time, even lifetimes, can be lost in relationships that are destructive, or relationships that are simply not supportive, and neither person is able to move forward into giving that which they are to give to the world. When relationships are not of the right match, not having the right set of attributes of giving support, much energy is spent in simply trying to keep those relationships alive in the midst of this lack of understanding, or even chaos. The energy and time that these relationships require takes one away from working toward one's own goals and sense of purpose. Therefore, it is important when one has a sense of purpose, that one examine all that is within their life to determine if it truly supports that which they believe they are to contribute.

Love supports. Love allows for the growth and development of the other. It provides the space when needed, the support when needed, the loving touch and assistance when needed, and the impetus for growth as it is needed. This impetus for growth can feel like the other is challenging, is perhaps even being unloving, yet this acknowledgement of truth, and the giving of truth to the other, is part of the support that is needed. All the relationships in one's life should be able to provide these forms of support.

A loving relationship will engage your whole mind, your whole being in a wonderful effort toward fulfillment. This engagement will provide the support and strength one needs to feel that sense of accomplishment in the world. It will be a source of joy, a source of mutual respect, and a sense of bonding and completion that cannot be found in relationships that do not have this mutual purpose. It will promote the growth of each individual, it will provide for the nourishment of each individual, and it will assist in the unfolding of the mutual purpose.

Love binds together that which is of mutual purpose. That is why there are those with whom one feels an intrinsic bond though one does not know them personally. When one meets someone and feels instantaneously that there is a bond, a connection, it is because at a deeper level one recognizes a common bond, a common goal. These intrinsic relationships are further nourished by becoming involved more personally in the pursuit of purpose and the enjoyment of mutual pleasures. As these intrinsic relationships are allowed to grow, they provide a source of stability and strength that cause each to flourish.

Love is the source of strength, of nourishment, of bonding, and of joy. It brings people into right contact and provides for mutual growth. This mutual growth brings about the fulfillment of purpose, and the world receives its blessing. Therefore, part of one's purpose is being in right relationship so that one can move forward to bless the world. All the world is blessed by the loving bond that unites the two in relationship.

As you find that which gives you a sense of purpose, consider that the relationships in your life need to support that purpose. Let this purpose prevail. Let yourself be supported by those relationships that strengthen and nourish your purpose, that you might have that experience of love, and that the world might be the recipient of that love.

The New Message of Love
I. Invitation to Love

The New Message of Love
I. Invitation to Love

Chapter Seven

Love finds fulfillment in expression. When one loves, it is not enough to be filled up. One must be allowed to overflow. This love fills one like a cup that continues to receive beyond its capacity, and once it is filled to capacity, it spills over into the world. Love is directed outward. It flows up to all who would receive. Love fills a vacuum that cannot be filled by any other means. Therefore, if one is not responsive to love that comes to them, they remain a vacuum. This vacuum will continue to desire fulfillment. If it is not filled with love, it will be filled with the glitter of the world. The glitter of the world is the fun, the material objects, the status, the recreational sex, the incomplete relationships that are prolific in society. As one continues to try to fill this vacuum with the glitter, one is continually hungry. It is like one whose diet consists of sugars, of fats, of those things that fill but do not nourish the body. Thus the body is always hungry, always crying out for the nutrition that would cause it to be full of health.

Much of the illness in society is caused by being filled with that which cannot fulfill. As one fills one's body with food that has been robbed of its nutrients, that has additives that are not healthy, that continues to deplete the body, the body desires more and more of that which does not fulfill its needs. Society is filled with those addicted to alcohol, to sugar, to those things which do not fulfill its needs. These addictions are the result of the body's crying out for more of what it needs, and yet being deprived. It is when one confuses the body's real needs with those perceived needs that addiction occurs.

This is also true of the spiritual vacuum. The spiritual vacuum cries for those things that would fulfill. It reaches out for love. When it is filled with those relationships that are unhealthy, with those things of the world that cannot satisfy, it may starve. In its starving, it becomes addicted to the things which cannot fulfill it. Thus society is filled with addictions to money, to sex, to youth, to acquisition, while the true hunger is for love.

Do not think that you can deny that for which your body and your spiritual vacuum have been created. It is like the roots of a plant reaching out for nutrients. It can accept only that which will cause the plant to grow. Therefore, when it does not receive the proper nutrients, the plant begins to wither and die. This is also true of the body and of the spiritual vacuum. If they are denied the nutrients needed for growth, they too begin to wither and die. There is much among the society that is needless. It is a walking death. It has the appearance of life, but if pursued, one can sense the emptiness that truly exists. The body becomes tight, the skin becomes taut, the eyes become hollow, and the lifeforce is not free to move throughout the body. When the spiritual vacuum begins to wither and die, one sees emptiness, one sees shallowness in relationship, one sees lack of purpose, one sees a philosophy that says, "Take it all now, as tomorrow it will all be gone," rather than, "Grow today, that you might become more."

When one is open to receiving that which one needs for the body and the spiritual vacuum, one grows like a strong, healthy plant. One is full of lifeforce, of enthusiasm, of positive desire, and of a feeling of being centered. When one is open to these nutrients, one is most aware of one's environment. One's sensitivity becomes heightened. As one eliminates those foods that are not a positive factor in their growth, one develops a sensitivity toward those foods, and it becomes difficult for them to be tolerated.

As one grows spiritually in Love, one is less able to tolerate the shallowness in relationships, the vindictiveness that one sees in the workplace, and the hatred that one encounters in the world. One is most sensitive to these things, and responds in a way that is disruptive. That is because as one becomes filled with Love, one becomes a most disturbing element in the presence of this hatred, of this vindictiveness, of this shallowness of relationship.

As the body thrives on those nutrients that it needs, the spiritual vacuum thrives on that which is fulfilling. The spiritual vacuum needs true relationship, needs meditation, needs one to be with Love. As one grows in relation to one's Higher Self, one increases in capacity to accept Love. As the capacity for accepting Love grows, one therefore is able to spill that Love into the world and becomes a channel for Love. Therefore, these steps for becoming a channel for Love are to become in tune with one's Higher Self; to open oneself up to Love; and to allow Love to flow through them into the world. This Love is a spiritual life force, an energy that cannot be contained. Therefore, once one has been filled to capacity, one cannot contain the Love that continues to flow through. It has nowhere to go but out into the world. When one has attained the level of being a channel for Love, one cannot return to the spiritual emptiness that one previously experienced without withering and dying spiritually.

Thus, Love opens one to the world, and once opened, that person must be most discerning. As one progresses on this spiritual path of life, one will have many new experiences. Each new experience will be both a challenge and an opportunity to allow God's Love into the world. These challenges and opportunities are never faced alone, for the channel for Love is never alone. As the person who is a channel for Love continues to receive Love, Love continues to flow through them. This Love accompanies them into every situation, and profound intuition provides the answers for dealing with these new experiences.

Therefore, the channel for Love must be most in tune with one's Higher Self and able to respond.

Love is the ultimate acceptance of one's Source, and this complete acceptance brings one to peace. Thus Love is a journey into oneself, a deepening understanding of all, and an awareness of one's unity with all that is. As one grows in this understanding, one realizes that Love is the force, the magnet, that brings all to that understanding of unity. That unity is the Universe. The Universe encompasses all, and there is no separation. It is only as each person chooses not to be separate that they are brought Home. Therefore your choice to become a channel for Love, to be open to intuition, to be accepting of Love and growing in that capacity, is the initiation into the journey Home.

Love is power. Its power is greater than any other. Once one has been claimed by Love, all other forces are powerless before it. Therefore, the channel for Love need not be afraid as Love overcomes all else. This is not to say that the person need not be discerning, for Love is a most disruptive force and one must always be protecting oneself from those who would strike out. Yet, if one follows one's intuition, if one continues to be filled with Love, one will overcome the world.

Jesus was a man who, through Love, overcame the world. His life is an example of the power and the magnitude, the magnetism and the disruption, of the power of Love. When one studies His life, one can see the force of Love in action, yet those who were unable to receive rejected Him. When one is a channel for Love, one will experience much rejection. Yet Love overcomes the world and this rejection must be seen in the light of the total occurrence. As one is rejected for Love, one is at the same time claiming the power of Love. For Love is greater than the experience of rejection. It is the world that is like a child, afraid and vindictive toward all it cannot understand. One would not be angry at a child for being afraid of what he does not understand. Thus one, too, is not to be angry at the world for rejection, for the world is simply rejecting and afraid of what it does not understand.

As the decision to be a channel for Love is made, that commitment causes one to burst out of the stage of being a bud into the stage of blossoming. It is this blossoming that will take one through the experience of fulfilling their purpose, and thus, return Home. The journey Home begins with the commitment to purpose, to being a channel for Love, and to following one's path wherever that path may lead. The journey of the channel for Love is the fulfillment of the spiritual vacuum. As the body accepts healthy nutrients and glows with the radiance of health, so the channel for Love glows with the radiance of the power of Love. It is this radiance to which others will respond. They will respond with acceptance or rejection. Neither is to be condemned nor judged. It is simply a response. Those who reject at this point in history will be those who accept at a future time. Therefore, when you experience rejection, experience it only as the other is not yet ready, and move forward with those who are ready to accept. When one is on the spiritual path, one must be able to release all who are not ready to respond so that one can be in relationship with those who may respond.

The commitment to the spiritual path brings the complete fulfillment of the heart's desire, and none can take away this joy.

The New Message of Love
I. Invitation to Love

Chapter Eight

The New Message of Love
I. Invitation to Love

*L*ove is the culmination of the journey toward the Source of one's being. Love chooses to follow that which it can only follow. It can follow nothing else. Therefore, when one chooses to live one's life in Love, one is choosing to return to God. Love is the greatest power on earth. It far exceeds notions of romantic love. It unifies all that it touches. In romantic love there is separation, there is great desire for union, and there are moments of union. Yet, the basis for romantic love is the projection of one's desires upon another. Therefore, union occurs only at brief moments when there is deep acceptance, or when there is deep belief that the other fulfills one's desires. The basis for romantic love is belief that the other matches those attributes one has chosen as important. Often in romantic encounters, one sees only those attributes one desires, and one fails to see other attributes that do not match one's required list and that need acceptance. These relationships frequently last for weeks or months until one removes the filter and sees beyond the desired attributes. At this point, one becomes disillusioned and frequently blames the other for being who they were all along. It is simply that one was perceiving the other through a filter.

In love, one sees without filter. One sees one's own strengths, one's own weaknesses, and accepts them. Thus by accepting oneself, one can see the other without a filter, see the strengths and weaknesses, and choose to accept all. It is this total acceptance without judgment that allows the relationship to develop into one of love. The joy of this kind of love far exceeds any experience of romantic love.

Romantic love is full of confusion and disappointment. It is full of a sense of being pulled up and down like a yo-yo. The acceptance and lack of acceptance pattern causes much insecurity, and at some point, turns to disillusionment. Marriages that are based on this notion tend either to stay together because of other bonds such as children or business, or accept that this is all there is. Those who feel cheated, who feel that there is more, will choose to leave that marriage, yet in many cases simply find other relationships of romantic love and repeat the cycle. When one can begin to see love differently, and can begin to look at a lover with total acceptance, one can come into true relationship. True relationship is not dependent on romantic love. It is dependent upon complete acceptance of self and of the other, and pursuit of common goals.

The combination of acceptance and common goals provides a solid basis for relationship. One cannot find true relationship by turning to the media for advice. One must go deep within oneself to know what it is their life must be about, and to go through a growth process of becoming self-accepting so that one may lovingly accept others. This process of self-acceptance takes time, and must be done by every individual. Those messages learned from when one was first born are piled high over one's head, and one must review and understand, and eliminate these judgments so that one can see another clearly. As one begins this journey toward seeing oneself without judgment, one immediately begins to open up the world in a way one has never seen it before. This opening up causes one to open to the love experience. As one opens up to the love experience, one then becomes a channel for Love. Thus the beginning of love is the acceptance of oneself.

Romantic love is a path that leads to disillusionment. This inevitable disillusionment results when one finds the other to have areas that they cannot accept. The judgments that render those attributes unacceptable are the same judgments that one has made upon oneself. In many cases, parents and other significant adults also made these judgments during the years of one's growing and developing. Therefore, the process of self-acceptance begins by looking at those judgments that were made when we were young, and determining the reality of those conclusions. One does not need to continue to judge that certain attributes are good and others are bad. One can see each as simply a way of being or reacting; a value, belief, or assumption; and realize that as the two people come together they will begin to meld, to forge new ways of thinking. Thus these attributes do not remain stagnant, and the two are free to choose the highest plane of functioning. When one can perceive the other with acceptance and love, one is therefore able to support the other, and in doing so, support the highest plane of behaving. This is not to say that one fits into relationship and tries to change another. This is a sign of lack of acceptance. Rather, by accepting oneself and another, the two forge new planes of seeing and behaving. Thus, love spills forth from the couple and blesses the world.

Do not think that your love relationship is for you alone. It is a source of creative energy, a generating station for love. As love develops and grows, the couple is filled to capacity, and this love overflows into the world. When one loves, one needs true relationship in order for that love to be generated and multiplied and cast forth into the world. Thus, love is far greater than the two could ever contain. It cannot be contained, and the positive energy that is emitted attracts other kinds of energy. Thus, love unites all who would love, and reunites them with the Source.

God is the Source of all love. God is the love. Love is God. Therefore, when you love, you are God in the world. The world is starving for love. In every place, love is needed. Wealthy and poor alike are starving. It cannot be bought; it can only be accepted.

Therefore, love comes through each channel for Love, and Love blesses and saves those who would accept it. True relationship is not limited to man and woman. True relationship is binding and commits one to the other. True relationship is fostered by the commitment first to God, and then to each other. It is important that both understand that the commitment, the devotion, must be first to God. It is in gazing upon one's Source together that one becomes united and the heart's longing is fulfilled.

Devotion must be only for God. It is this shared devotion, this pursuit of common goals and purpose, that form the highest kind of relationship that one can express in the world. One is not limited to only one such relationship, as one may also find that relationship with one's child, one's parent, with one's friend; yet the relationship between man and woman must not be violated. Therefore, commitment of a physical nature must be more sound, and must be forever limited to the partnership. One cannot enter into true relationship lightheartedly. One must enter filled with devotion, desire for the highest form of relationship, and be willing to be totally accepting of oneself and of the other. Thus the romantic highs one has associated with love have no place in true relationship, as one is making a serious commitment of one's life to one's Source, to one's purpose, and to another. The love that results will be far greater, far deeper, far more lasting than that which is romantic. It will not be characterized by the illusion and disillusionment of romantic love where one repeatedly falls in and out of love. It will be characterized by genuine bonding, by commitment to a higher Source, and by the deep desire to resolve differences so that love may continue to flow through.

Love gives of itself through those who would accept. Those who accept, however, must be ready to give up all, to follow. They must become Disciples of that Love. Thus to be in true relationship, one must be a Disciple of Love, of the Source of one's being, and one must be prepared to give up all in support of that love. This does not mean one will give up all, as one needs much to be able to navigate in the world; yet it means that one must be willing to examine and remove anything that is a blockage to that love. As one commits to one's higher purpose, one is then drawn into that arena where one can experience true relationship. One must be willing to move into that arena alone, as it is only by moving alone that one has the possibility of a true relationship. One must be willing to be alone, to trust, and to move forward alone, so that one becomes strong in order to be able to accept and maintain true relationship. Thus, the moving forward of love is preparation for true relationship.

The acceptance of the spiritual path is made within oneself. Although others may join in combination, one truly makes this decision alone. It is only when one can make this decision alone that one can go forward and attract to oneself those things that are needed to bring this purpose to fruition. It is the willingness to take this step that propels one into the path of love. Once propelled, one cannot return. Like the internal parts of the bud, once the casing has broken, one enters into another reality from which one cannot return. One is then to bloom, to bring its complete essence to the world, that one can experience complete fulfillment, can bless the world, and continue on the journey Home.

The step toward right relationship is a step in trust that all one's needs will be provided. Let your desire be for God, and all else will be added.

The New Message of Love
I. Invitation to Love

The New Message of Love
I. Invitation to Love

Love brings all who would participate to the Source of their being. Love invites. Love challenges. Love fulfills. Love rewards. It is the nature of Love to transform one toward the fulfillment of their deepest and highest goals. When one encounters an invitation to Love, one must empty oneself of former notions of the meaning of Love. It is essential that one be able to move away from the association of Love with romantic love, and be able to move into the understanding of Love as the fulfillment of the heart's greatest desire. At the core of the heart resides the understanding of true meaning. At the core, one experiences knowing at its deepest level. One may not be able to express this intellectually, may not be able to understand or to verbalize its meaning, yet it is truly known.

The core of one's heart is the deep recognition of all that is, and all that has been. It can be brought forth to conscious understanding by involvement with a person or thing that activates this intuition. This activation begins a process of returning one to one's true self. Therefore, Love invites, Love recognizes, Love activates and returns one to one's Higher Self.

The acknowledgement of one's Higher Self brings one into a level of more conscious preparation for fulfilling one's purpose. One has been in preparation for a very long time, yet this preparation has been done at a more unconscious level. At the moment one's intuition is activated, and one gets in touch with one's Higher Self, one begins a more conscious level understanding of one's purpose. Those who are dedicated to Love, who are consciously following a spiritual path of Love, are brought into contact with those for whom it has become time to have this intuition activated. That is why, when one is on a spiritual path, one often does not understand why one must go in a direction, or must be at a specific place and meet specific people; yet this is all part of the plan. This plan brings people into contact with those who can initiate them into the spiritual path, which will bring them to fulfillment of their purpose, and a return to their Source.

The activation of intuition is the beginning of the conscious invitation to complete one's purpose. One can encounter those who activate their intuition in many different areas, many different activities of life. It may be within their job, within their family, with known friendships, on vacation, at any moment. When that moment occurs, one's life is changed. One can never return to the former life and be the same. One will see differently, and it can be most confusing if one is not brought into an understanding of the meaning of this change. Therefore, when one is on a spiritual path of Love that activates profound intuition in another, one must be most aware that with this activation will come much confusion and, in some cases, a sense of being threatened or afraid. One needs to be ready to provide that care, that understanding, that responsiveness that is needed.

The responsibility to respond to this intuition can only be with the person whose intuition has been activated. This person must look for support from others, but must look inside for direction. This activation puts them in touch with their Higher Self, and intuition moves them to behave, or to respond, in certain ways. At this time there are those who leave relationships, even marriages, who say, "I don't understand why I must do this, but I must." Who look for ways to justify their actions and cannot find adequate reason; who may look to blame others and yet not find a reason to blame. It is a period of much confusion externally; yet internally, one knows that one has encountered a point in life from which there is no returning.

One may experience guilt as one feels that society is judging them. One may encounter judgments and ridicule from those who do not understand, yet one will move forward with new understanding. It is important to connect with others of spiritual understanding who can provide assistance. This community will support the other without judgment. It is important to seek support to care for one's self and to know that one is doing what one must, even though there is no conscious understanding why this is occurring.

When Love invites, it can be a most persistent invitation. Love is the greatest of all magnets. It draws to it those who would respond. When one cannot respond, one goes through much internal confusion and self-doubt. Fear may cause one to strike out or to protect. Yet Love will issue another invitation at another point, and eventually all will respond.

When Love calls, it is important to realize that nothing will remain the same. One's relationships, one's position, one's use of time will all begin to shift away from old perceptions into new ways of service. It is during this period where there is great internal shift that one can be most uncomfortable, one can feel shaky, and one reaches out to those who can provide assistance. As one goes through this period of time of great internal shift, one begins, after much internal exploration, to stabilize. As one stabilizes, one begins to feel more grounded, and more ready to step forward into their purpose. At this point, the things of the past seem less relevant and have begun to fall away. Those things that remain must come into alignment with one's purpose. Therefore, time and resources needed to fulfill one's purpose must be in alignment, and there must be reconsideration of all else. As one goes through this period, one does much releasing. This release can be most uncomfortable for others. Yet once one has made the decision to accept the invitation to Love, one cannot return. As Love fills the vacuum that only Love can fill in each person, the energy, the need for fulfillment, becomes most strong. One desires to step forward into that purpose. That desire for purpose and for fulfillment are all that truly matter. Therefore, everything in one's life is brought into a point of service with one's purpose.

As one begins to stabilize, one can then be more supportive of others whose intuition has been activated, and who can accept the invitation to Love. Thus the circle becomes wider, and as it grows, more people have their intuition activated and receive the opportunity to respond to Love. It is this ever-increasing response to Love, to the fulfillment of one's spiritual purpose, that will return all to their Source. Thus, Love is the circle that never is broken, and always is increasing in size. As it increases in size, it continues to encompass all, and to surround the planet. Love will bring peace to the planet. Yet, peace will not be something that the planet will experience all at once. It will be an increasing response to the activation of intuition and the invitation to Love.

Love moves forward, and touches, and unites. It is the energy that will bring the planet to peace. Yet, its force is most disruptive. For those who are able to accept the invitation to Love, there will be much unity, both within oneself and with others. Yet for those who are unable to accept the invitation, there will be much fear, disruption, and striking out. Those on the spiritual path to Love must be most capable of this understanding, and must be able to be accepting. It is not for one to judge others as to their acceptance, or lack of acceptance, in response to Love. It is for one to offer the invitation and to go forward, gathering all who choose and are able to respond. Thus, positive energy draws positive energy, yet negative energy also draws negative energy; and it is these forces that can be most disruptive and can clash. That is why when Love invites, much destruction is left in the wake of the invitation.

To be on a spiritual path of Love, one must be able to accept that this is the highest will, that this is God in action, and that one must accept the plan if one is to be a part of it. Therefore, it is the returning to the Source, the magnetism of the power of Love, and the repulsion of the negative energy, that is all part of the plan. Yet Love is the greatest force, and Love eventually brings all to Source. Therefore, when one accepts the invitation to Love, one accepts the journey to spiritual fulfillment and to God.

As you receive the invitation to Love, move forward into the circle that it might expand, that it might unite, and that it might bring peace to the world.

Love condenses all that is, and changes that energy into a mighty force. Love integrates, unites, and brings into service all that one has known, all that one is able to do, and creates energy that propels one into the world. As one begins to discover one's purpose, one begins to realize that all one's life experiences, whether good or bad, can be used to further the work of Love. As one begins to move forward and discover each new step, each new piece of the puzzle, one realizes how a part of one's life fits that piece of the puzzle. The purpose for one's life is uncovered in stages. These stages are like pieces of the puzzle. When one completes what one must do in one piece of the puzzle, one begins to uncover another piece. As this new piece is uncovered, one sees how other experiences in one's life are a part of the new puzzle piece. Thus, if one considers the flower, all that has occurred in the growth process within the stem moves forward through the stem to be drawn into the world as part of that purpose.

Those instances in life that were considered tragedy, that were considered a failure, can now be used for good. Thus a tragedy is never truly a tragedy as there is a positive purpose to be gained; and failure is only another life experience that is brought into fulfillment of one's purpose. It is not that tragedy comes into lives in order to form purpose, but that purpose is allowed to be fostered and supported by these life experiences. Therefore, positive can always come from negative experience or what one perceives to be negative.

One must also realize that what one interprets as tragedy is not in God's Plan a true tragedy. While the loss of a child can feel most devastating to the family and to the friends, that perceived tragedy is an event where the child's purpose for being in the physical world at this time in history is complete. Leaving at a time others would consider most unfortunate creates the opportunity for growth in those who are affected. Therefore, from a Higher Perspective, it is not truly a tragedy. It is the fulfillment of the Plan, as this event propels those affected forward along their own path.

Each person, at any point in their own evolution, has an opportunity to choose how to interpret and respond to a life event. They may become depressed, they may give up, they may become bitter; or they may choose to take the wisdom from that experience and transform it into a contribution to the world. Choosing to interpret a life event in a manner that can bring forth love into the world causes not only one's purpose to be fulfilled, but also continues to bring forth the purpose of the one who left this life on the planet at a time perceived to be premature.

One must be most able to surrender to God to realize that all happens when it is supposed to happen. One does not truly have a choice in this event. While one may promote healthcare, one may provide emergency services, prevention and intervention will not be effective if it is indeed a part of the Plan that one should leave at a preordained time in order to complete a purpose. Thus it is those who remain behind who must be most willing to surrender those they love in order to be a part of the higher plan. Society often perceives this as a great inequity. It perceives that all should be entitled to a lifespan of a specific amount of time, and that those who leave the earth-plane sooner than this timespan have indeed been cheated out of the opportunity for more life experience.

It is only when one can begin to see life as a continuum that has many experiences, some on the earthplane and others not, that one can see that one does what one needs to do for a prescribed length of time in order to fulfill that purpose. Therefore, if that purpose is complete, or promotes another's purpose by a certain event, that is what one must surrender to, as this is a part of God's Plan. All are not guaranteed a similar lifespan as all do not have the same purpose. One's purpose goes through much evolution. Therefore, in one lifespan, one may complete that aspect of one's purpose only to complete another aspect of it in another lifetime. That purpose is always ongoing. When one nears completion of one's purpose on the earthplane after many lifetimes, that purpose to brought to consciousness. As it is brought to consciousness, one must make a choice. One must choose either to follow one's purpose, or one will choose not to follow one's purpose at this time. Yet, one must complete one's purpose to return Home.

It is not for those who are on a spiritual path to become saddened or afraid for those who choose not to complete their purpose, as they will complete it at another time. They are choosing to return and to move through these opportunities and choices again. Therefore, those on the spiritual path who have made the decision to fulfill their purpose must move forward with those who also choose to fulfill their purpose. Therefore, those who are on that spiritual path must be most committed to their purpose and to one another. There are few on the spiritual path who are at a point of conscious awareness of their purpose, yet they are most essential in moving everyone forward. They move forward those in spiritual families from beyond, and they move forward those who are less evolved but who are gaining new understanding. Thus the intuition of one on the spiritual path activates the intuition of others. Some will respond to that activation. Others will choose to fight inwardly and deny it. Yet all who have been touched have been activated. That is why the activation of intuition is most disturbing. There is great discrepancy. Some will follow; others will react negatively, or in fear, or run away. The person on the spiritual path must be most cautious, as they must be ready to encounter many different reactions. These reactions may be directed toward them personally. Therefore, once one is on the spiritual path, one must forever be most discerning.

When one is on a spiritual path, one begins to realize that one has great understanding that is beyond what is generally known. This can be somewhat frightening, somewhat isolating, and somewhat confusing. It can leave that person on the spiritual path in a position to need to be with intuition in order to know what to say, and how much to say, about that which they know. They have great understanding of the need to fill the vacuum in their hearts with only that which can fill it, their Source. They can see others suffer, and understand the source of suffering. They know that there will continue to be much upheaval in the world. And while they, in their personal self, desire to become part of the world, to deal with the world, they know they must move into their higher self and accept that which is needed for the world's growth and evolution. Therefore, one has bifocal vision. One sees the world as one always did, yet one sees the world from a higher perspective and knows that one must accept and love the world, and use their life to serve the world's needs.

As the world moves forward in its evolution, it will begin to prepare for a great joining. This joining will be with other evolving worlds. There is much change occurring within the earth. People are coming together in ways that before were not even considered. They are living together, they are moving together, they are creating new forms of communication and living that, only a short time ago, could not have even been conceived. This is part of a planetary evolution that will bring about a greater joining in a universal community with other worlds.

The earth is experiencing much evolution. Other planets also are experiencing much evolution. At a point in that spiraling evolution, there will be a time of great joining. At the time of joining of these worlds, there will need to be much understanding of how one comes together with those who are different. Thus, the preparation for this greater joining is the coming together of people of different nationalities, cultures, and backgrounds. As this acceptance is allowed to flourish, one will become ready to move into the next step of the evolution, which is the joining of many worlds.

The person on the spiritual path is most aware that they are viewing the world's evolution from a higher perspective. They are able to recognize the needs in the world, and to serve the world, that it might move forward in its evolution. As people become consciously aware of their purpose, they realize that their purpose is truly to promote this evolution. Therefore, each on the spiritual path is most important toward the evolution of their planet.

The evolution of the planet will bring about much opportunity for joining. It is in joining oneself in self-love, and joining with others of diverse lifestyles, cultures, and background, in joining with one's purpose, and in joining with one's Source, that one becomes ready to join in the larger planetary community. God is One. God is Source. God is Energy. God is Love. God is Peace. God is Intuition. God is All. Therefore, when one unites with another, one unites with God.

Love is the rejoining of one with one's Source. Love brings about the realization of the separation one has created, and therefore allows one to eliminate separation and be one with one's

Source. Love is the rejoining of all to God. Peace is attained when one has become enjoined. Therefore, Peace is the returning of all to God. Intuition, Love, and Peace are the trinity by which God is experienced. Yet, God is One, and all are enjoined to be One with God. When we move from separation to God, we are part of the great energy of God, and we will be part of the magnet that draws others. Thus, as each step is taken, all are drawn into unity with the Source.

The New Message of Love
I. Invitation to Love

The New Message of Love
I. Invitation to Love

Chapter Eleven

The New Message of Love
I. Invitation to Love

𝒯he Love of God beckons that all might follow. It is like a beacon in the night. It draws one's attention away from those things of the world, and causes one to focus on things from beyond. As one begins to shift one's focus, one finds that this beacon becomes a mighty magnet drawing them toward the Source. The Source is light energy, is Love. As one allows oneself to look toward the beacon, to focus on the light, one is drawn away from the things of the world, and one learns one can only find peace as one is moving toward the light. As one begins to make this step forward to begin to commit to the spiritual path, one must leave much behind. The initial steps can be most painful, as one has many attachments. As each one is released, one is able to pull away and to move forward into the light.

It is in this moving forward that one becomes purified, that one becomes most sanctified, that one becomes most holy in One's sight. It is this sanctification that enables one to move forward with a life dedicated to Love. As one moves into this light, one finds much peace, much fulfillment that one could never find within the world. It is those things of the world that have held them captive for so long, yet have left them empty and searching. As these things are released, the vacuum one has is filled with the Love of God. This vacuum can only be filled by Love. There is no replacement that is fulfilling. Many would try to fill this vacuum with experiences of the world, with relationships, with material goods, yet these do not fill the vacuum that can be filled only by the Love of God.

As one moves forward, one begins to take on other qualities. These qualities can be discerned by many. One is often not aware of these qualities they now possess, yet their presence causes disruption wherever they may go. This is not necessarily a negative disturbance, yet it is something that causes others to become aware that there is something changing within them. It is this internal change that creates the new tension and can be manifested outwardly in ways that are most interruptive. The person on the spiritual path must be aware that they are a channel for Love and that this Love can create much turmoil. As one moves forward, one leaves a trail behind that is most apparent to others. This trail is a trail of those who have been affected. Many will be drawn to this person. Others will be repelled and will not be able to join for some time. Therefore, as the person on the spiritual path moves forward, the effects of this Love can be seen.

One moves forward on the spiritual path, activating the intuition of those with whom they come into contact. This activation is a strong internal shift. Many have been prepared to join this person on the path, yet will be unable as the internal shift will create fear and they will be frightened away. Others will find the Love emanating from the one on the spiritual path to be most fulfilling, and they will desire more as they experience this Love. Therefore, those who come into contact with one on the spiritual path will be drawn toward them, or will be repelled. It is important when one is moving forward into the light, that one note those who are able to follow. They are to be drawn into the fold. They are to be nurtured and cared for and supported as they begin to take that first step following their Source. Therefore, the one on the spiritual path becomes like a link in a chain. As that link moves forward, others join behind and follow.

As you move forward in this commitment, many will be touched, many will be changed, many will turn away. Those who come must be cared for and encouraged to follow. Those who are repelled must be released with love. All will eventually join, as Love is the most powerful source. Yet some will have greater resistance. The one on the spiritual path is a great leader as well as a great follower. One cannot lead without being also a follower. As one follows the guidance they receive, they will bring strength and courage and direction to those who desire assistance. Therefore it is most important for the one on the spiritual path to receive daily guidance that their path might be clear; that they might not lead anyone astray; that they might move the link, and therefore the chain, forward.

As one moves away in perspective, and can see what is occurring, one can see that these lights are drawn together and are being drawn Home. There is much movement to bring this joining. It is occurring in many places within the earthplane and in other worlds. This great joining with the spiritual families will begin a greater joining amongst families until all are joined. This joining is felt in your planet by nationalities coming together, by the barriers breaking down, by the breaking down of social systems, and the joining of languages. It is most essential to assist in this joining as many will be most resistant, and in their resistance is their pain. This suffering will continue until all can join. Therefore, to bring peace into your world, it is essential to bring Love that all might be enjoined.

The love of God is the greatest force. The peace of God is the resolution of resistance. Therefore, as one joins, one finds peace. It is those who are on a spiritual path who will bring about peace in your world. It is by being a channel for love and peace that one affects those around them, that one causes both some to follow and some to resist. Yet it is in gathering those who will join that one contributes to peace.

As one joins, the move toward the Source is most strong. It draws, it purifies, it sanctifies. And those who continue to be brought to the Source continue to move outward as channels of peace and love. Therefore, any link affects any other link in the chain. This is how love will multiply in your world. It will grow; it will envelop your planet. But this will take much time. Many must join. Many must become channels for peace and love. Therefore, as the disciples of Love, you must move forward into the world, and you must assist in that joining.

God will be experienced as Intuition, as Love, and as Peace. Yet God is All. God is One, and all are One. It is only by your thoughts of separation that you separate yourself from that one Source. Therefore, as you begin to accept that you are a part of that one Being, of that one Source, and as you allow your love for self and others to emanate into the world, you will assist in bringing peace to all.

Love is the magnet that draws all to its Source. It is like the rays joining the sun. It is like the dew returning. It is like all that has been created returning to the Source of Creation. Allow your love to flow to all. Do not limit its expression. Even as you are discerning, allow love and peace to flow from you. Keep in constant awareness that you are a Disciple of Love, and that is your reason for being on the planet at this time, that you help restore all to God. As the Disciple of Love, you are most valued. The love of God that flows through you can only be restricted by your lack of acceptance. Therefore, accept yourself knowing that God loves you as you are, and allow this love to ever flow forward. Love is the invitation to the feast. Peace will be with you through eternity.

The New Message of Love
I. Invitation to Love

The New Message of Love
I. Invitation to Love

Love resolves all dilemmas and promotes the growth of each individual. It is the resolution of dilemmas that allows one to spring forth into their Purpose. Those who are prepared to move forward into their Purpose are rising out of dilemma. This dilemma may be in a relationship, the expectations of others, what society has taught that is required, or personal fears that must be confronted. Yet, the resolution of the dilemma leads one to Love. As Love draws one toward it, one moves out of that dilemma. It is as though the power of Love is stronger, and the painful transition is the time when one is pulled in both directions. When one is yet being pulled, one has oneself clinging, or being clung to, and being strongly drawn in another direction simultaneously. This is most painful. This conflict that is created must be resolved for one to begin to have any peace.

The conflict of the dilemma can create much emotional pain and suffering, much physical pain, even illness, until one is clear what it is one must do. When one returns to the relationship, or the situation that they have been holding on to, they are most dissatisfied. While they may feel initially that they have done what was good to do, what society expected them to do, what family expected them to do, they soon become filled with a sense of disillusionment. It does not ring true with them, and they know they have missed an opportunity.

When the choice is made to go into the direction that is drawing them, and they accept this force of Love, they are first slowly drawn, then propelled into service. This service is their fulfillment. It will bring about a fulfillment that cannot be brought by the old situations. Therefore, now that they are new in the Love of God, and the service of God, they cannot return to the old, as they will no longer belong. It is that once this door has been closed,

The New Message of Love
I. Invitation to Love

it is locked. The future is bright with new opportunity for service. Yet, one must not look back. One must take that step with courage and with much faith. The resolution of the dilemma of being drawn away from those situations where one was most entrenched will bring about inner peace. This peace is the result of following Love. Therefore, Love is the invitation that draws one away, and this invitation creates much conflict and disruption.

Once it is clear what one must leave behind, one must take that step into the future most boldly. One must say, "I cannot be here any longer. I need to go and do what it is I have been prepared to do. I will always love you. I will always treasure the memories of our times together, yet I must go." It is this bold step into the future that allows one the opportunity to be free. Freedom is having no choice but to follow Love. Therefore, in choosing to be a Disciple of Love, one is free from all other constraints. That is why one must be willing to walk away from all that is conventional. They must be willing to leave family, to leave friends and home, to go to wherever it is they are needed, to do what it is they have been uniquely designed to do. As one makes this commitment, one realizes one's assignment. This assignment is one's Purpose. Therefore it is the commitment that must be made before one can know what it is that one must do.

The Love of God brings joy that is without comparison. There is no joy like unto that joy. That joy fills, fulfills, and delivers one to that place where all is peace. The one on the spiritual path must be most serious, most intent upon completing their purpose. They must be willing to step forward into the unknown. They must be willing to trust that all that is needed will be provided, and they must be able to not allow the criticism of the world to compromise their purpose. Therefore, one moves forward alone.

One does not look back. And one has the faith that they are never alone, and that their needs will be met.

The Channel for Peace and Love is most beauteous to behold. Their light is pure. Their desire is pure. Their heart is filled only with God. Yet, there are many steps on this path toward that purification. One is always moving forward; one is always becoming purified. Yet one is sanctified when one commits. This commitment is most essential to be made publicly. It is this public commitment that creates the support, the foundation, for one to continue forward. As many are committed, they form a community of Disciples, and these Disciples are then launched into the world. The Disciple of Love will need to experience much travel as there is much sorrow, much pain, much hate where Love is absent. Therefore, one must be willing to go to where Love is needed and bring Love. God moves in the world through people. God does not have hands other than those of His followers. Therefore, it is the hands of the Disciples that create, that support, that nurture, and that supply; that the way may be known, that the Invitation may be offered, and that those who are receptive may join.

Do not think that this purpose is for oneself alone. This purpose is for the world, for it is the world that benefits. The loving relationships that are established benefit the world, for God emanates from them through Love. All relationships where love abounds allow God to move in the world. Therefore, love becomes the vehicle, the inspiration, the invitation to God. Love chooses those who are ready to follow. Love offers opportunity, yet Love is always moving forward. Therefore, when the opportunity is not taken, that opportunity does not come again for some time. That is why there are many lifetimes; there are many times to respond. As one evolves, one becomes more prepared to be able to accept this call. Therefore, those who are Disciples of Love are called and have responded.

Let your life be a response to the world's need for Love. Let Love fill you, inspire you, direct you, and lead you, that all whom you encounter might be called. As those who are able to respond move forward, more are gathered to God. Therefore, the joining that occurs brings us to the place we know as Home. Home is a distant memory when one is in the world. Home is a yearning for something that one cannot fulfill. It is only in the acceptance of Love, and the receiving of Peace, that Home is experienced.

Allow Love to become manifest, that all might know and receive that which awaits them.

The New Message of Love
I. Invitation to Love

The New Message of Love
I. Invitation to Love

The New Message of Love
I. Invitation to Love

Love is the answer to the difficulties of the world. Love brings together those that would unite in a way that is most profound. This unity is a most joyful union for those who are participating, yet its real benefit is for the world. The world longs for, desires, hungers for, union. That union can only be brought about by the acceptance of Love into one's life. It is this Love that unites one to one's Source and unites one to all who have previously joined. Thus the union of two is in reality the union of many.

When those who are joined continue to grow, this union becomes stronger, more magnetic, more profound. It is like a massive moving of Spirit that begins to envelop the planet. When those who are joined from beyond join with those who accept Love, and thereby return to their Source, this union encompasses your planet in a most profound way. As this union grows, and continues to grow in the future, one becomes aware that there is movement in other parts of the universe. This movement is a greater joining, and is occurring in all worlds.

Love is the magnet that is returning all to God. Love can be experienced in any world and beyond. This experience is like a great returning, a great joining that evolves, develops, and surrounds each being. Yet there is the opportunity for choice, for resistance and denial in every being. Returning to one's Source is a choice. It is a choice to accept an invitation to follow Love.

Love soothes and challenges, molds, and takes apart. This sun beats down, gently sways and profoundly moves all that it engenders. It brings all to both turmoil and peace, as the turmoil must precede the acceptance. Once one accepts this invitation, one then begins a process of continual preparation which is most defined. It requires the one who has accepted the invitation to pare down, to eliminate all that is not in alignment with this new life.

Some will make an initial acceptance but will not be able to move forward. This is most painful as they feel most inadequate, afraid, and in fear of rejection. Yet it is not rejection but lack of readiness that has occurred. They must be nurtured. They must be allowed to know it is acceptable to wait, as in the future there will be another invitation. Yet all who would accept must be encouraged to follow. This path is most difficult, yet the way is most fulfilling. This fulfillment cannot be accomplished in any other manner. So the one who has accepted, has accepted opportunity for complete fulfillment as a step in the journey Home.

There are many who are accepting this Invitation in all worlds. Many more are not yet ready, and must be invited and encouraged to join. Thus, the Message of Love moves forward calling all who would follow, and making Disciples of Love who then, in turn, invite all to follow. This is occurring in all worlds that the universe might return to its One Source.

Do not think that Love is for only the one who accepts, for the two who unite, or for the spiritual community, as Love is for everyone. Once one accepts, one takes on the commitment to prepare oneself so that one can then invite others to join.

Returning to one's Source is one's ultimate goal, yet most are not even aware that this is their goal. The world has many distractions. It has its own rules, its own status, its own hierarchy, its rules for behavior, its own rituals and religions. Yet they are not the path to one's Source. The path to one's Source can only be found through the acceptance of Love.

The New Message of Love
I. Invitation to Love

The Universe is reaching out to all who would accept. The Invitation is given to all. None will be rejected, yet the requirements are great. One must prepare to hear the Invitation. One must prepare for acceptance. One must be continually in preparation to receive the direction one must follow.

As one moves along each step, one is always at risk of not being able to take that next step. One is surrounded by temptation, by those things of the world that are most distracting and provide some relief and gratification. Yet they do not fulfill the true longing in one's heart. It is only after one has become most disillusioned, that one has completed the preparation for the Invitation. Thus the preparation for the Invitation to Love is disillusionment of those things of the world.

The Invitation to Love will not be heard by those who are still distracted. They will become afraid, for at a deeper level, they know. They will become most threatened, and may strike out at the one who invites them to join. Thus, the one on the spiritual path must be continually aware of the disruption which is a result of the Presence they carry, and they must be most prepared to deal with these results.

As one goes forward on the journey, one begins to grow in awareness of the union that is occurring throughout the Universe. It is as if the rays of light from the sun were reversing and returning to the Source. Thus, as one moves into the light, one becomes absorbed into the light, and joins all others. This great reunion is occurring now, and is the beginning of the greater joining of the universe. Thus, Love calls the individual. The individual who responds joins with others who are responding, and that response is part of a universal return to God. As one dedicates one's life to fulfilling one's Purpose, this Purpose serves the world by serving as an Invitation to Love. Though this invitation may manifest in many ways in many circumstances, it is all a part of the Invitation to Love.

Love binds all into the sea of energy that is God. It is this joining of all spirits that increases this power. God is Power. God is Energy. God is Light. God is Spirit. God is Love. God is Peace. God is Source. God is One. Therefore, in joining, all are a part of the Heart of God.

Allow Love to call you, guide you, direct you, enfold you, and bring you to everlasting peace.

The New Message of Love
I. Invitation to Love

The New Message of Love
I. Invitation to Love

Love provides the direction for those who would follow. Love is a wondrous force which attracts and pulls all who would follow toward Home. Home is the eternal peace of God. Home is the goal of all in all worlds. All belong to the Source.

Love is the instrument of peace. Love is the tool by which one can create, one can move forward, one can experience peace. Love is like a difficult path through a beautiful garden. While one is surrounded by the beauty, the joy, the serenity of the garden, one must toil diligently to remain on the narrow path. The path is filled with many twists, many turns, many challenges. It is not that one completes a challenge and one is finished, but that one must continually take the next step. The next step unveils a piece of the Plan. This piece of the Plan is like a tiny piece in a giant puzzle. As one receives the next piece of the puzzle, one gets another view, another perception of the reality of the Plan. Yet the Plan is so large, so universal, that one can never see it all as one is on the path.

The spiritual path requires much faith, much courage, and much determination. It must be one's complete desire. One must desire it above all else. As those things appear along the path which would cause one to stumble, one must be full of commitment to God. One must accept assistance from beyond to be able to take the step that moves one beyond that obstruction. Therefore, one is always climbing. As one takes the next step, one finds new joy, new life, new fulfillment. Yet as that is occurring, one is also preparing the next step. Therefore, one is never finished growing; one is never finished moving forward.

Those who choose this path choose it because only it can fulfill them. That is why one must be most disillusioned with the distractions of the world to be able to make this commitment. As one moves forward beyond the distractions, one attains peace and joy that one did not know was possible. Yet one also receives challenges that must be overcome.

One's commitment at this point is most essential, as without commitment, one will go off the path. As Love moves forward, gathering those who would respond, not all will be able to fulfill this commitment. Those who are able must continue. They must not stop, as this would pull them, also, off the path. One must not become overwhelmed with concern for those who are unable to complete this commitment, as they will be given future opportunities to commit. It is not that they are rejected; it is that they are not yet ready, and must continue their preparation. Therefore, let no one take you off the path.

The garden is most wondrous. It is filled with that which the heart most desires. It fills the huge vacuum that resides in all, and can be filled only by God. Therefore, think not that the reward is small, for there is no greater reward.

Love is a most disturbing force. It is not always gentle. It is not always kind. It can be most disruptive and can create much upheaval. The upheaval in the hearts of individuals is reflected in their auras, in their crimes, and in their lack of caring and concern for one another. Therefore, one must not think that when Love invites, there will be peace. There will be much upheaval. Yet those who are able to accept, who are committed to follow, will receive the peace they most desire.

Love is the most powerful force. Love is God-in-action. God is powerful. God is all-consuming. God desires all to return Home. Therefore, the magnetic force that is God is most powerful.

Love divides. It divides those who can accept from those who are not yet ready. This division will cause much upheaval in personal lives, in religions, in cultures, and in your world. Yet, Love will, in the end, draw all Home. It is only a matter of time as to when, in their evolution, each person chooses to join. This joining is most wondrous. It is a joining of those beyond to one another, of those in the world to one another, of those in each world to one another, and of all in all worlds, and beyond. This magnetic force of Love is calling all Home. All are being invited to return to peace. Therefore, the contribution of the one on the spiritual path is to accept the Invitation to Love, to accept the peace in their lives, that they might bring peace into the world.

The person on the spiritual path therefore becomes a Channel for Love and Peace. As they become channels, peace comes into your world. Peace is not the cessation of war; peace is the acceptance of God. Therefore, allow peace to enter, allow peace to flow through you, that your world might come to a total experience of Peace.

Love is the Invitation. It is being offered to all who will follow. Allow Love to draw you into the journey that leads Home.

The New Message of Love
I. Invitation to Love

Chapter Fifteen

Love draws one away from the distractions of the world into a sanctuary of peace and service. Love causes one's focus to change, and one's desire for God to increase. As this desire increases, one desires to serve God in the world. This service is most needed by the world at this time, and also as preparation for the joining of all worlds. As one's desire nature unfolds, one feels most at peace. One feels as though one has finally stopped the restless searching that has been with them for so long. This searching has created a sense of unrest, and in some instances, conflict in relationship.

As one begins to step forward into fulfilling their purpose, one feels as though they are beginning a whole new life as they follow another road. This road is full of promise, yet there are many difficulties in navigating. One must be able to navigate strong turns, be able to avoid obstacles, be able to climb steep mountains, be able to stay in control going down steep mountains. The spiritual path is not unlike the challenges of the world, yet the challenges of the world do not bring fulfillment comparable to that of the spiritual path.

As each obstacle is encountered, as each turn is navigated, one comes upon much beauty. This beauty is felt internally. It is a deepening of the commitment, a deepening of the desire nature, a deeper experience of God. As one enters the stillness through meditation, one comes into deeper God experience. This experience is most holy. It is entering one's Higher Self into the God experience. It is not to be feared. It is most peaceful. It is unlike any other experience of peace, for the world's sense of peace is resolution of conflict. Yet this peace experience, for the one on the spiritual path, is the experience of God.

The New Message of Love
I. Invitation to Love

The world cannot offer this experience. Peace is that which is most desired by your planet. It is talked about, yet it is not something that can be accomplished through the world. It must be found through Love. Therefore, by accepting the invitation to follow Love, one accepts the opportunity to experience peace.

When one enters into the silence, one is drawn forward slowly. One does not need to be afraid, as the God experience is most beautiful, most gentle, most powerful, most fulfilling. Once one has tasted this experience, one cannot return to the world's definition of peace, for it is far too inadequate to serve them.

The experience of the peace of God draws one more deeply into the God experience. Yet, the distractions of the world are ever-present. As one enters stillness through meditation, one needs to allow the mind to become quieted. One must choose to stop thinking of the things of the world and, for a time, move away from those things of the world that are most demanding. When one makes this conscious decision to focus, to enter the stillness, one must desire to enter. When one's mind is still racing with thoughts of the world, one cannot enter stillness. Yet, in stillness one finds resolution to conflict, one finds answers to those things of the world, and one finds internal peace. When entering the stillness, one decides to set aside the issues of the world, yet may find it most helpful to pose a question for which one is seeking answer or resolution.

Then, let go of the question and focus on stillness. Allow yourself to enter. As you enter, there will be a sense of emptiness at first, and after some time, a sense of being filled. That sense of fullness may be experienced emotionally and even physically. It is not to be feared, as it is gentle, and loving and fulfilling. As one lets down one's guard, one's barrier to God, one allows oneself experience of the God presence.

This will happen as slowly as each individual needs, so that one does not feel one is becoming overwhelmed. As one moves forward on the spiritual path, one must enter stillness often. For it is in stillness that one is given the strength to go forward, the resolution to desires of the personal self, and the answers to concerns.

The one on the spiritual path must make daily practice their primary focus. Everything else must become secondary. Therefore it is not enough to say, "I will do my spiritual practice if I am not too tired, if I am not going out, if my children don't need me, if my husband doesn't want to watch TV." One must make the decision that spiritual practice is the most essential part of their life. They must set aside regular times in the morning and at night to be able to maintain the focus of spiritual purpose. Therefore, when one is on the spiritual path, one becomes most self-disciplined. It is this self-discipline that allows them to progress.

The Disciple of Love puts God first in their life. It is their desire first to serve God, and secondly to serve family, profession, the world. All of one's life must come into alignment with their service to God. Service to God is done through spiritual practice and fulfilling of spiritual purpose. Therefore, the one on the spiritual path has made the decision to belong to God. Belonging to God means following God as one's higher authority, choosing God over all else, and being most diligent in practice. One will receive assistance from beyond when encountering those situations where one is being asked to put others before God. When one is on the spiritual path, one must learn to overcome the guilt one has learned regarding responsibilities and the world.

There will be many times when others will make requests where the one on the spiritual path will have to follow their higher guidance and deny the request. This can be most painful, and if one is not most cautious, they can leave the spiritual path at this point.

One must accept that those who are making requests have other resources from which to draw. One must allow them the opportunity to turn to these other resources. These resources are made available to them, and they are receiving assistance from beyond. Therefore, the one on the spiritual path must let go following this refusal of assistance, knowing that other assistance is available.

Your society has taught people to accept guilt. Guilt is often the way one comes into feeling obligated. When one feels obligations to others, one must look at the source. Is serving this person in this way a part of my spiritual purpose, or am I doing this out of a sense that I must because of former obligations, and to avoid feeling a sense of guilt?

The person on the spiritual path will encounter guilt as they reject these requests for help, yet they must understand that guilt is of the world. It is what the world teaches. Therefore, this is not from God. God does not teach guilt. God promotes desire. That desire is to fill the vacuum in one's heart which can only be filled with God, and this creates desire for service. Therefore, the one on the spiritual path must be most discerning about all requests. They must ask if this request is in alignment with their spiritual purpose. Those things of the world that can take one off the path are often what one has been taught are good things to do. Taking care of others who are capable, putting others first, moving forward with professional commitments, are all things that are considered good in the world, yet can cause one to go off the path. When one enters stillness, one sets aside those requests, those obligations, those commitments. One can ask for guidance, and then enter the stillness, knowing that they will come to resolution.

Spiritual practice, then, is necessary for one to be able to remain in alignment with one's purpose. Spiritual practice increases understanding, deepens desire, and allows for the experience of the peace of God. Therefore, the one on the spiritual path must be most diligent in this self-discipline. They must put spiritual practice above all else.

Allow your life to come into alignment with spiritual practice, and inner conflict will be resolved. Allow yourself to enter stillness, and the experience of God will bring you peace. Allow yourself to be a channel of Love and Peace, that the world might be blessed and be brought into Love and Peace.

Therefore, one is far greater than oneself alone. The influence of one who is on the spiritual path toward bringing peace to the world is far greater than one could be alone. It is as if one's power for peace were magnified a thousand times. It is God working through the person on the path that will bring the world to peace.

Let your life be in service to God, that all might know and experience everlasting peace.

The New Message of Love
I. Invitation to Love

*L*ove is a fire that consumes all. It makes the recipient its own. The one who responds to Love becomes the child of Love. The child of Love serves gratefully, knowing that their life is in service to the highest order. That order is its Source.

When one is in service to one's Source, one must be able to accept that others will often be unable to accept them. One must be able to assume leadership at a level that allows for non-acceptance by others, yet where one is not dissuaded from what one knows. It is leadership born of Love that will bring the world to peace, yet that leader will not know peace in its traditional sense. That leader will know upheaval, disruption, and the pain and sorrow of personal loss; yet will also know the highest level of unity one can achieve while in the world.

One moves forward as if one's being were in two different planes: the plane of the world is where the service is performed, where the Message is brought forward, where the leadership is assumed, where the support is given and received; yet the higher plane is where one receives guidance and direction. Thus the great leader is also the great follower. As one becomes a Disciple of Love, one must be both a leader and a follower. One must be a leader in that one must realize that they will be surrounded by much upheaval; yet, they must remain firm, remain strong, and grounded to their inner knowing. They must be able to separate themselves from the world to receive guidance, and to be a great follower.

The one who sees with the eye of Love, who sees as if they have bifocals, must be able to see those who are able to accept, and those who are unable. It is as if when one looks through the higher part of the lenses, one sees with Love the Higher Self of the other. Yet when looks through the lower part of the lenses, one sees how that person is manifesting. This manifestation is a result of the personal self, or a result of the Higher Self. The Higher Self will be able to accept the message of Love. The personal self must make a choice. Therefore, if the personal self chooses to accept its Higher Self, its higher intuition, and accept Love, this will be its manifestation. If it is unable to accept, it will be manifested in ways that are most disturbing, and may result in feeling threatened and striking out. Therefore, the one who is a Disciple of Love must continue to be most discerning.

The Disciple of Love must function on both planes. They must be able to function in the world and remain most grounded. Yet they must be able to separate from the world to become filled up, to receive guidance, and strength, and the ability to go back into the world as a leader. One who is a leader must have a highly defined sense of self, must be able to move through the lack of acceptance of others without losing one's own identity. Therefore, it is most essential that self-love be cultivated. As self-love is cultivated, one is more able to love others, accept others, accept one's own limitations and the limitations of others, and move forward with their purpose.

Therefore, Disciples of Love must continually care for themselves, must continually reinforce those positive means of personal care, and must believe in their own worth. They must believe that they are worthy as a child of God, that they are a servant of Love, that they are a disciple and a believer. Therefore in order to lead, one must both be a great follower, and be able to take much personal care of oneself.

The leader will always have another leader. That is why they must be a follower. The leader, the Disciple of Love, will have both leadership in the world and beyond. The leadership in the world will be most human, most able to respond on a personal level, yet will need time away to reflect and receive. Therefore, when one has a leader in the world that one is close to, one must be able to allow that leader time to be alone. The Disciple of Love must continue to be strong, must continue to move forward and depend on their own inner strength and resources, and the strength from beyond to move through this period.

The child of God sees wonder all about them. They see the beauty of the world in its colors and its fragrances, in its movements and sounds. They see the beauty of people in their caring and their giving, their love and sharing, and they see the beauty in themselves as they receive from beyond and give that which they have received. Therefore, the Disciple of Love, while able to discern all other manifestations of disruption and disturbance, continues to see beauty all around and within. It is this double vision that allows them to move forward. For if they focused only on the disruption that is created by the presence they carry, they would turn back. Yet they are able to experience the disruption and still see the great beauty all around. Therefore, they are in a position to hold up the beauty of the world for the world to see.

Disciples of Love must be able to see God's beauty manifest both in the earth, and beyond. They see the beauty of assistance. They see the beauty of the hierarchy of levels of movement toward God. They see the beauty of joining. They see the beauty of the Plan for all to join and return Home. In the world they see the beauty of love, caring, giving, sharing, color, sound, movement, light, and they allow this beauty to move them forward. Disciples of Love are able to maintain their sense of leadership because they are able to see, and to assist others to see, that the darkness that much of the world is in is a result of their inability to see the beauty that truly exists. For the others, it is as if their reality, their paradigm, let in very little light. They see limitation, they see disease, they see fear. They see death as a limitation. They are unable to see assistance and light and beauty. Therefore, the call of Love is the call to move into that light that one might see this beauty.

When one has moved into that light, and has begun to enjoy and assimilate this beauty, one must remember that those around them are not able to see, they are not able to hear, the assistance provided. They are not able to see the beauty of joining. They see only that which they fear: the ultimate destruction of their personal self.

The Disciple of Love holds forth that beauty for all to see, holds forth that promise of the world's flowers, as it moves through its preparation, as it bursts its casing, and as it opens and shares its fragrance with the world.

It is this vision that must be presented to the world, that the world might choose to move into the light. Once one is in the light, one forgets the darkness, one moves out of fear and limitation, one fosters health, and growth, and desire for continued movement.

The channel for Love and Peace therefore becomes a Disciple of Love by providing leadership to the world. The Disciple is one who takes the Message, lives the Message, and moves the Message where it can have an opportunity for acceptance or rejection. It is this Disciple, this child of God, who is most blessed, as their life is blessed by receiving and by giving.

As the one on the spiritual path moves forward, becoming first a channel for Love and Peace, and next a Disciple who actively moves the Message of Love into the world both through their life and their Message, they are most holy. Life's treasures are not measured by what they accumulate of the world, but what they receive from beyond and contribute to the world. Therefore, let your treasure be both your gift to yourself, and your gift to the world.

The New Message of Love
I. Invitation to Love

Chapter Seventeen

The New Message of Love
I. Invitation to Love

Love is most splendorous. It is the wonder, the magnitude, the depth, the breadth of what is possible within the human experience. There is no other experience that can compare. Love is the world's most powerful force. It can overtake, overrun, and destroy fear, hate, doubt. There is nothing it cannot heal that is of an emotional nature. Love heals emotions so that the physical might also be healed, as the disease of the body is but a manifestation of the distortion of the emotions.

Love's force enters when one becomes open. It cannot enter that which is tightly closed. Therefore those among you who have erected walls to keep out the light of Love live in darkness. Their darkness is most frightening to them. They are like animals that have not seen daylight in a long time. Their vision is distorted. Their perception is limited. They seem only to be on a treadmill that is ever going in circles. This treadmill does not take them forward. It does not bring in new experience. It is not fulfilling. Yet those who choose to live behind these walls feel a safety in knowing the limitations within the darkness. They fear the light. They fear what will happen next. They fear new experience. They fear those who are not behind such walls. Therefore, when they encounter one who is not living behind these walls, they become most threatened.

The denial of that which they most desire, the Love experience, creates feelings of hate, resentment, and defeat. Their perception is therefore that one must take and enjoy all that one can in the moment, for that is all there is. It is a perception of great limitation, and they perceive themselves only as being in a meaningless vacuum. They attach themselves to any stimulating experience, as this momentarily erases the pain of the emptiness within.

When they encounter a being filled with Love, they become most angry at the contrast with their own lives. They throw verbal darts. They challenge serenity. They attempt to overpower. They may verbally discredit. And they move away from that one who is most threatening. If they continue to stay in the presence of Love, they will choose to hide, to avoid, to maintain their own internal existence. This occurs when they are in a position such as that of employment, where they must come into contact with the one who is a channel for Love and Peace. Yet they are simultaneously drawn to that person, for they are beginning to open to the Love experience. This is most frightening. The walls they have erected are most fragile, and can be shattered by Love. Thus, their security is shattered, for their security is based upon a perception of limitation.

Their response to the channel of Love may be most negative, most undermining, and most challenging. At the extreme end of the spectrum, they may become violent and attempt to physically destroy. At the other end of the spectrum, they may deny, they may undermine, and they may avoid the one of Love. They may respond in any combination of methods that lie between these. If, however, their wall has any cracks and begins to crumble, they may feel most vulnerable; and, at the other end of that spectrum, they may follow. Thus, the possibilities of one who encounters Love may go from physical violence to total acceptance. The one on the spiritual path who is a channel for Love and Peace, who is a Disciple of Love, must be aware of all the possible responses. They must be most discerning, yet they must not block that Love from coming through.

Love destroys defenses, shatters walls, and draws all who would follow, to it. Yet there are those, who by their own free will, will choose not to follow. They must wait for future opportunities to join, for they are as yet not ready. The one who is a Disciple of Love must gather those who are able to join, must nourish them, and must assist them in being propelled into the world to draw others to their Source.

The splendor of Love is all glorious and magnificent in its beauty. It is the light out of darkness, the fullness of experience, the fulfillment of purpose. In whatever form that purpose may take, it is a part of the trinity of Intuition, Love, and Peace. Therefore, it is the purpose of each to play a role in the returning of all to God. Spiritual Purpose is fulfilling that for which one has been designed. There is no purpose that is unimportant. All are needed. All are designed to return one Home, and to return the world to its Source.

It is not that one should look at another who is fulfilling their purpose and compare, or feel that one purpose has more importance than another. There is no hierarchy of purpose. There is joining. There is shared purpose. There is shared desire for God. There is shared experience. When one is fulfilling one's purpose, one must be in relationship with those who are also fulfilling that purpose. Therefore, the purpose for which one is designed is the role that one plays in bringing together the culmination of the final return Home. Peace is the result of fulfilling that role, that purpose in the world, and bringing others to Peace. One does not bring peace to others; one brings others to Peace. Therefore, the journey of Love brings one to eternal peace.

The journey of Love encompasses other existences, other realities. It is not limited to human experience. It is the journey that one begins with acceptance, and follows through one's ascent into joining. Thus, the rays that return to the Source are the journey of Love. The journey is complete when the Source is the total experience. While one is in the physical world, one can have moments of God experience. One can move into one's Higher Self for brief periods of time. This occurs during meditation. One can also move into a bi-focal position of being in both the Higher and personal Self. At the end of the journey Home is complete God experience.

No one has seen God, yet many have had experience of God presence. It is when that experience of God presence is one's only experience, that one has completely returned Home. That is why one can have experience of Home in the world. One brings that experience to the world, and the world has the experience of Peace. The channel for Love and Peace will have that experience, and that experience will propel them along their journey of Love. There is no other experience in any plane of existence that is as great as the God experience.

The acceptance of Love is the beginning of God experience in the world. Therefore, accepting and drawing all to God is the only true peace in the universe. All worlds are being drawn into that God experience. All are joining.

Allow Love to be the Invitation to the universal experience of Peace.

The New Message of Love
I. Invitation to Love

The New Message of Love
I. Invitation to Love

Chapter Eighteen

The New Message of Love
I. Invitation to Love

*L*ove is the most essential element in the component of life as it is manifested in the world. When one moves beyond this world, they are joined with those of their spiritual families from whom they came, and to whom they return. Yet while one is in the world, one has no recollection of this previous experience.

While one is in the world, one moves freely, one responds to situations, one chooses one's path, and one makes choices based upon one's values. Yet, one does this without remembrance of previous lifetimes, and the experience between lifetimes. Therefore it is Love which is the invitation to return to that Source from whence all life originated.

Love is the invitation to receive one's true calling. One's true calling is to return Home. Thus, Love is the invitation, the response, the acceptance of the journey which leads to eternal peace. When one is in the world, one is capable of experiencing peace, yet one must focus on a return to Peace, as peace is not within the consciousness at all times. When one is in the world one has many challenges, and choices in how these challenges will be resolved. As one makes choices, one is always learning. One learns by the consequences of their actions. Yet there are those who have been unable to move beyond negative consequences, and begin to learn from their experiences. In those instances, there are continued opportunities for learning.

When one is able to move beyond those obstacles, to learn what it is they are to learn, and to move to the next step, one is moving forward in the journey of Love. This journey is comprised of many steps, yet at each level, one receives much assistance in moving through that step. The person moving through life has the opportunity for choice. They can accept or reject that assistance. When they reject the assistance, they have no other support for moving forward. They can become quite stuck in that level of experience. Therefore, it is most advantageous to reach out, to accept that Invitation to Love, that one might receive much assistance and move forward.

One is always receiving assistance in the world, yet this assistance is brought into much deeper reality when one makes a conscious choice to receive it. All the benefits of the Spiritual Family and Teachers from beyond are brought to assist the one on the spiritual path. Therefore, while it may appear there is little assistance within the world, even at times no apparent assistance, there is always much assistance from beyond.

The one on the spiritual path may at times feel most alone as they gaze outwardly in their world for those who would assist, and it is often at these times that they face most difficult challenges. Yet they have the inner resources to propel them beyond anything the world can construe. The great leaders of the world had reliance upon these other resources. These resources are beyond, yet come to them from within. That is why they were able to move forward, to face all that the world could bring upon them, and yet go forward with their plan. They relied upon resources from beyond by looking within.

The person on the spiritual path is never without those inner resources, yet they are always at free will to choose not to rely upon them. When they choose to be self-reliant only, to feel that they do not need other assistance, they become most vulnerable to going off the path. Therefore, spiritual practice, looking within, and depending upon profound intuition, bring one through many obstacles on the journey of Love to the point of return. That point of return is the return Home.

The New Message of Love
I. Invitation to Love

Home is the spiritual Home. This Home is filled with much love and relationship that is beyond what can even be dreamed of while one is still within the world. While one is within the world, one has deep longing for intimacy, for union, for unity. Yet this is the memory of the spiritual Home for which they are truly yearning. One can join with one's spiritual family and one's Teachers while in the world. One can experience that level of intimacy called union when one is in relationship with one's spiritual family, and with one's internal strength. Yet, one will find complete union, complete peace, when one returns Home.

Home can be experienced in the world by those who are able to choose Love, follow their spiritual practice, and be open to the experience of inner knowing. This inner knowing is an experience of the God-seed. It is the return while in the world to one's Source. One's Source is always available. Therefore, Home is available in the world. Peace is available in the world, yet it is only by coming to Peace that one has this experience. One does not bring peace to the world; one brings the world to Peace. Thus the Message of Love is a Message of the return to Peace.

Love joins. It joins all who would respond. It brings unity, union and the beneficence of intimacy to one in a way that is beyond one's greatest fantasy. Yet it is only through much spiritual practice this can be reclaimed. One cannot take short paths to this reclamation. It must be done by moving one step at a time. Therefore, it is in spiritual practice, in following those steps that are revealed to one, that one moves into this most beautiful experience.

Love challenges and supports. It denies and comforts. It gives and takes. It shakes away all that is nonessential, and makes room for the receiving of all that is needed. Therefore, as one experiences the falling away of those things that are no longer needed, one opens oneself to receive all they will need to move forward on the path and to fulfill their specific calling in the world.

Each is led to receive their calling by experiencing their own inner guidance, their own inner reliance upon their Higher Self, and those beyond who assist. It is as they become more reliant and trusting that they are more able to receive and to serve. Therefore, they must be able to be vulnerable, full of faith, able to trust that which they know, yet cannot see. The results they are able to witness give them the courage to continue to move forward in trust. Thus, as one on the spiritual path experiences that they are provided for, they gain the courage to take more risks knowing they will be assisted from beyond.

The person who is a great leader with great inner resources, who is able to lead others in positive directions, is able to rely on these resources from beyond by looking within. They serve as an inspiration to others to be able to move forward, as their lives exhibit courage and faith. They provide assistance by giving witness to that which can occur when one is able to depend on spiritual assistance. Yet it is still the responsibility of each one on the spiritual path to make that choice.

Love is the Invitation, the Journey, the Way. There is nothing that is more powerful, more beautiful, and its magnificence can only be experienced by those who are willing to accept. This acceptance is the first step of the journey Home.

When one chooses to accept Love's invitation, one begins the magnificent journey that leads to the fulfillment of the desire for union. One's heart is fulfilled. All longing ceases. One is one with Peace.

The New Message of Love
I. Invitation to Love

The New Message of Love
I. Invitation to Love

The New Message of Love
I. Invitation to Love

Love is the foundation for all true achievement in the world. Love supports, leads, and guides from beyond. Love is that which brings all that is of Love to fruition. It is this foundation that provides the one on the spiritual path with the strength to move forward, to move through each step, to move through fear, and to receive the joy of fulfillment.

Love brings one to the brink of true commitment to one's Source. This commitment allows one to respond to one's calling in the world. That calling is the role one must fulfill to move forward, and by moving forward, allow all to take the next step. All are coming together now at this point in history. Those in other worlds are taking comparable steps. They are making commitment; they are returning to that Source of all life.

The return to Source is the deepest desire of all lifeforms. These lifeforms are manifesting in those who are human, and those who are beings designed to be able to prosper in other conditions. A simultaneous drawing forth of all lifeforms is occurring. You are a part of this return, yet it is essential to understand that you, individually, have free will to choose not to respond. Not to respond is not to join. Therefore, it is only by responding to the Invitation to Love that one begins the journey which unites all who would follow, and returns them to the Source.

Those who are able to respond will find their lives most full of beauty. They will have inner beauty that radiates into the world. They will become channels for Peace and Love. They will provide the invitation for others to join. Thus, it is by joining that one is in a position to offer the Invitation to Love. As one moves forward in this journey, one moves through many challenges and much beauty. Yet even the challenges provide fulfillment, for it is in the accomplishment of the steps that one moves closer to God.

The New Message of Love
I. Invitation to Love

This journey will take one to unknown places, to unknown spaces where much is new, much is curious, and one must be able to follow one's profound intuition. It is this inner guidance that will assist one to move forward on the path. Do not think that the spiritual journey is for the traveler alone. It is for the benefit of all. Therefore, all receive the benefit of those who would respond to the Invitation to Love.

As one moves forward, one realizes that one is becoming worthy of being the sacrifice for God. This is the highest position one can attain, as it is in giving that one receives. Thus the one on the spiritual path who reaches that level of accomplishment, is the one who gives all. One does not ask, "What will I receive? What does the world have for me?" but, "What may I give? What gifts may I contribute to the world?" Thus one's life is a life of contribution or sacrifice.

Sacrifice does not mean that one loses one's life by violence, but rather that one gives all that they have. All that they have includes their strengths, their weaknesses, their joys, their sadness, their knowledge, their role to the world. Therefore, as one becomes God's sacrifice, one receives all that the Universe is.

Think not that you have come to receive the glitter of the world. You have come to contribute your knowledge and your specific gifts. It is in giving these gifts that one realizes fulfillment in the world. Fulfillment is the experience of Home.

There are no short cuts to this attainment. One must be willing to move forward in faith, trusting that one is guided and supported from beyond. Thus, Love is the foundation that supports one in one's journey to Peace. Love is the foundation that lifts all who would respond, that they may return, and in returning, find eternal Peace. Thus, Love is the foundation, the invitation, the way, to Peace.

Consider that you are now invited. Consider the opportunity to respond. Consider all that will be yours upon responding. Consider how your life can be a blessing to the world. And if in that consideration, you find yourself drawn, open yourself to Love. Love does not ask; it invites. Love does not plead; it challenges. Love does not fall away; it provides eternal support. Love will bring each who respond, Home. Thus the acceptance of Love is the beginning of the journey Home.

As you move forward in contemplation of the acceptance of the Invitation to Love, allow yourself to be open to that which is within you. Look within and ask, "Am I to follow? Is this for me? Is it time to take this step?" If your answer is positive, step forward with courage, knowing that you will never be alone. Love is stronger than the earth upon which you move. It is stronger than the forces that would pull you away. There is nothing as strong as Love. Therefore it is that foundation of Love of which you can be sure, and it is the only foundation that is certain.

As you deliberate your response, consider that not only you, not only your world, but that all the universe is blessed by your acceptance. Move forward with confidence that you have chosen that which is of God, and you will be eternally blessed.

The Invitation to Love is the greatest opportunity one receives in one's lifetime. Therefore, it is only a matter of moving through one's internal resistance to receive all that is most glorious.

The New Message of Love
I. Invitation to Love

You are invited to join. Let nothing hinder your response. Love will be your constant support. You will never be alone.

The New Message of Love
I. Invitation to Love

The New Message of Love
I. Invitation to Love

The New Message of Love
I. Invitation to Love

Love is the trumpet that calls all to participate. It is the sound of the music of God that entreats all to follow. Love is the leader that moves gracefully to each, gently inviting, lovingly challenging all who would, to respond. Love is the most melodious of sounds, yet it is most intrinsically related and most deeply connected. As it reaches into the one who is receiving the Invitation, it pulls them in a way that is beyond their understanding. The music connects with the vibrations of the soul and there is a resonance that cannot be explained. Once that resonance is experienced, and that God-shaped vacuum begins to receive its song, no other song is as beautiful. All other music pales by comparison. Therefore, one is able to respond and leave behind all other things that once were so important. One can only respond to that deepest calling.

The music of Love fills the heart where all else has been unfulfilling. It soothes, it resonates, it vibrates to the music of the soul. It fills the vacuum, and all else pales by comparison. Thus, when the Message is given to follow, those who receive the Invitation and respond must move away and move forward. It is this Invitation to respond to one's deepest nature, for that nature has been prepared for a specific calling. Once one begins to respond, one is most amazed at how perfect the Plan appears. It is as if their heart's desire has been fulfilled. All that they have deeply longed for now begins to have expression. Therefore, the longing in their heart begins to experience resolution.

When one's calling is known, one finds new devotion, new desire to follow, for Love is the strongest of all magnets. It is stronger than hate. It is stronger than any force that would destroy. As one responds, one experiences the peace of God. The challenges of the world become less frightening. Those things that seemed large, now seem small. The glitter of the world loses its luster, and one's heart becomes most devoted. This devotion makes one a powerful channel for peace and love, as others see the devotion, and know of a higher Source and calling. One never leaves that calling behind; it is always within. Therefore, in the most usual of circumstances, others are being touched by that individual. The God-Presence they carry emits a power and presence. The lack of understanding of the recipient does not negate the power they feel. They are able to realize at a deep level that they are having an experience that is most important, yet they may not yet have the conscious understanding to be able to relate this to their experience. The one who is a channel for Peace and Love continues to move forward, touching all who would respond. Those who can respond know that they have communicated on a level that is beyond their ability to understand. This can begin to translate into conscious understanding. This understanding may not occur for quite some time, and the one who is the channel has already moved beyond; yet the lives they have touched have been changed.

When one is able to respond to Love, the music of life is more beautiful than any they have ever heard. The music surrounds them, uplifts them, and they feel cherished. It is as if God surrounds them with all that is beautiful, even while they are able to see the views of the world that they must address. It is as if they move forward surrounded by a large sphere that protects them, that nourishes them, that surrounds them with light, that all might see their beauty, that all might hear the music, and respond.

Thus, Love is a powerful invitation, and the one who chooses not to respond has much internal conflict. They are full of doubt and fear. They question their own capability. Some are not able to respond at this time. The channel must move forward, knowing that God is present with the one who cannot yet respond, and there will be more preparation and assistance from beyond to help them to respond at a later time.

Love causes much division between those who respond, and those who are not yet ready. This response can be most volatile, yet the channel for Love must not look back. They must move forward with confidence knowing that the Presence of God is always with them.

As one responds to the Invitation, one's life comes into alignment with one's calling. One becomes even more beautiful. The focus on Love, on forgiveness, on caring, makes them like a beautiful light in a darkened world. Their light shines, that all might see and respond. The music of their soul activates the music in others. Therefore, Love unites, Love lifts up, Love lights the world, that all might see.

Out of darkness, out of lack of understanding, out of emptiness, out of depths, one moves into the light, the music, the beauty, the Love of God. One's calling is most uniquely suited to one's nature. It is as if one discovered oneself, and finds the discovery most amazing. It is as if a package has been opened, and inside is the most beautiful gift of light; the gift one always desired, yet desired without understanding. For one does not know that one is empty until one is filled. One does not know that one is silent until one resonates. One does not know true beauty until one sees beyond the glitter. It is in the experience that one finds understanding. Therefore, one must step forward in faith, trusting that the harmony they desire will be provided. One will not understand, yet one must be able to step beyond understanding. One must put aside fear, and allow oneself this great experience. Do not think that one sees and then responds. One responds, and then sees. Therefore, the Invitation to Love must be received and accepted with faith. For without faith, one cannot take the necessary step that begins the process of unfolding.

The Invitation to Love is the challenge to take a step, on the faith that one might see and experience a different world; and that through this experience, one might contribute the gifts they have brought with them so that the world might be blessed.

When you step forward with commitment to Love, your life will begin its transformation. The transformation will bring harmony, light, and peace into your life. Open the door of your heart that the music might resonate, and that you might follow.

Love is the music of the Universe joining all with the Source. As the Universe becomes reunited, Peace will be known by all. The Invitation to Love will result in the reunification with Peace.

The New Message of Love
I. Invitation to Love

The New Message of Love
I. Invitation to Love

Love is the Source of all beauty, of all that is worthy of God. Love reaches down and touches all that it beholds. It desires to provide that sustenance of the soul that is eternal. Love knows only Love, and therefore, its magnetic power draws only the love it receives. That love it receives is the acceptance of the Invitation to Love. Love is so expansive that it is never completely filled. As it draws more and more to it, it finds that it is capable of holding more than before. Therefore, it will never be complete until all are within the fold.

Love is a giant vacuum that draws all toward fulfillment, yet it draws only those who would choose to be drawn. As this mighty vacuum moves forward, it reaches into all areas that contain those who would respond. Therefore none are left behind who choose to return.

As this giant vacuum moves forward, its reach encompasses all worlds. All worlds are being drawn to return to the Source. The universe is far more vast than man has yet discovered, or that man will be able to ponder until well into the future. Man can only dream of what may be beyond their ability to travel. Yet humans are only babes in the eyes of the Universe. The Universe is magnificent. It contains those beings that are suited to each environment. They are found on the surface. They are found deep within. That is why even your explorations have not revealed that which truly exists, for that which is inherent in each world is only that which is suited to that specific inheritance.

As you begin to ponder what may actually exist, you will feel like you are moving through a science fiction movie. You will be able to proceed, to envision, to hear in ways that are beyond your scientific understanding. That will make it very difficult for many, as they live within a belief of scientific principles which excludes that which We are able to tell you. Therefore, for those whose minds are able to be open to other research such as that which We provide, they will be able to move and to discover that which truly exists. Yet, those who are bound by belief systems based upon rudimentary means of scientific proof or evidence will be limited in their own ability to make scientific judgments. Therefore, the dichotomy which will exist in your world will be between those who can only accept what they are able to prove by their limited knowledge, and those who are able to believe based upon experience. This new spirituality is experience-based, and will not fall within the realm of your scientific understanding. Thus it will be that the great division of the coming generations will be the division between those whose belief systems remain relatively unchallenged, and those who are able to step beyond scientific evidence, and move into experience.

Already the experience of those who have stepped out of their belief system far surpasses that which can be scientifically known. Those who have moved into new realms must be most discerning, as they could be persecuted. Therefore, they must practice their beliefs, yet with discernment. They must draw others into the experience with caution. They must share their experience with the understanding that it can only be to the level that the other is prepared to accept. Yet, as with all new understanding, there will come a time when it is no longer possible to hold back that which one knows. What one believes may limit one. What one knows can never limit one, for it is always evolving. The one on the spiritual path who is open to experience will, almost from the very beginning, be at a level of experience beyond what those who are held within belief systems can accept. Therefore, when one enters the spiritual path, one becomes unburdened, as those who are not ready to move forward must be left behind.

The New Message of Love
I. Invitation to Love

The one on the spiritual path must be brave, must be trusting, must desire understanding beyond anything else. Therefore, the great unburdening which they experience will be to leave behind all that cannot follow. This may include relationships, possessions, security; yet the desire for understanding must be filled.

As the one on the spiritual path moves forward into experience, the experience will continue to nourish them, yet they must follow a curriculum that nourishes them. They must be in the presence of their Source daily to receive this nourishment. If they are not, they are like a young seedling that develops with so much promise, yet withers and dies without proper nourishment. Therefore, once one has made the commitment to the spiritual path, one must continue forward or one's spiritual life, and hence one's entire life, will wither and die. The glitter of the world can never provide the nourishment that the soul seeks. If one returns to the world, one will never experience that same satisfaction. Therefore, the one on the spiritual path must be firm in commitment, must be sure upon making the commitment that God is what they most desire.

Think not that you can make only a partial commitment, as you will not be able to withstand all that you must endure to stay on the path. Therefore, the response to Love, which is commitment, must be made with great desire and faith. The fulfillment of that commitment will bring one to Peace.

The channel for Peace and Love is joined with channels from many worlds, all worlds within the Universe. Thus, the channels for Peace and Love move the rays forward to their Source, and increase the magnetic pull Home. The reclamation of one's understanding is what allows one to accept this spirituality based upon experience. This new spirituality is another step in the evolution of the return of all to God.

Your planet will experience much divergence. Its small wars of a tribal nature will escalate into division over spirituality. Yet, this cannot be avoided. Therefore, those who hear the call must hear the importance of receiving this Message, as the rejection will cause them much internal disturbance. They will see, but they will not understand. They will reject their understanding. They will challenge and will not find answers within their belief system. They will be lost. Therefore the Invitation being extended by Love is to move into spiritual experience.

The commitment one makes to accept this Invitation moves one forward into deep spiritual experience. Therefore, it is important to give serious consideration to the Invitation to Love, as one may move into that experience which brings one to Peace. Love is the Invitation to spiritual experience that goes beyond scientific proof or current religious belief. Therefore, one must move forward, trusting in God that the acceptance of Love is the provision for Peace.

The New Message of Love
I. Invitation to Love

The New Message of Love
I. Invitation to Love

Love is the unending joy of knowing one's Source. Love abounds in the presence of God. It is this presence that fills the longing in one's soul. Love cannot be surpassed. It is the music of the universe brought to earth. It is the colors of the rainbow in the rain. It is the reflection of the sun in one's own eyes. Love fills one to capacity and beyond. It lifts one when one is sad. It carries one when one is tired. It blesses one when one is lost, and it cherishes one as it brings one Home.

Love is not glamorous, but strong. Its strength goes beyond the walls of defense that hide the frightened. It goes beyond the safety one knows into the challenges of the unknown. One is never alone when one is with Love. Love raises the lonely, supports the weak, and brings the empty to wholeness. It restores all that is needed to bring one to eternal peace. Love is the most powerful force in the universe, yet Love knows only Love. Therefore, one always can choose to reject Love.

In the emptiness of longing, one reaches out for something that will take away the pain, and that is only alleviated by Love. Therefore, Love fulfills, Love carries, Love cherishes. Love takes all who would respond and makes them Its own. Once one belongs to Love, one is filled when they would be empty, strong when they would be weak, fulfilled when they would be full of desire. Love knows no strangers, as Love draws all Home. One cannot be unworthy of Love, for Love only desires Its own. It is, therefore, only by deeming oneself unworthy that one chooses to reject Love.

Love of self is the foundation for all Love, as it is only by acknowledging our worthiness that one can accept Love. Therefore, one must be able to move out of the pain of unworthiness to accept all that is in store. One must base one's love of self not on accomplishment, not on status in the world, but upon the knowledge that one is born of God, one is eternal, and one is here to learn and to contribute.

Think not that you can earn Love, as you are already worthy. Think not that you will be rejected, for only you can reject. Love cannot reject. Therefore, it is one's response to the Invitation to Love that moves one forward to everlasting Peace.

The joy of Love transcends all happiness that the world can give. The glamour of possessions, of status, of relationships cannot compare. When one is on the spiritual journey, one will find those relationships that will support one's path. Therefore, once one commits to the journey, one will be joined by others on that same path.

This relationship born of mutual commitment and mutual purpose is from beyond. It was established prior to one's earthly existence, and will continue beyond. Therefore, one on the spiritual path recognizes that one is never alone. One is assisted by one's Teachers, one's Family from beyond, and by right relationships established before one entered the earthplane.

All of earthly life is but a journey toward Home. Yet the journey is cluttered by distractions. One may find, at the end of one's earthly journey, that one must return to continue the work they have begun. Thus one may have many lives in many worlds, as one learns the lessons needed to move forward. These lessons are steps that must be taken to move forward on one's path. Much of the preparation is done before one encounters the Invitation to Love. This Invitation represents their next step.

Once one makes the commitment to follow Love, the steps on one's journey become more conscious. One begins to see the steps as a part of spiritual fulfillment. One begins to understand that one has come to the earthplane to learn, and to contribute to the world. Therefore, think not that the world is about glamour. These are only distractions. The world is about being where one can learn and contribute, and move forward in their journey Home.

When one is taking a step, one may face much doubt, fear, and temptation. One must be most committed to be able to move forward. Therefore, one will find much fulfillment as one moves through the step and prepares for the next step. Love will carry you through the journey, yet it is necessary to be most devoted. Once one begins a spiritual path, one's devotion must be to God. That devotion must represent one's highest priority. Therefore, all else must come into alignment with that priority, which is God.

Joy is the product of following Love. It is the heart's fulfillment. It brings one to everlasting Peace. Let all your prayers be that God will make you worthy of this journey, that you may bless the world and be in Peace.

The New Message of Love
I. Invitation to Love

Chapter Twentythree

Love is the foundation on which will rest the salvation of your world. Love will provide the basis for all decisions that must be made. All decisions will be based upon one's desire for God that can go beyond tradition, accepted belief systems, and lack of spiritual experience. Those decisions, where one commits to the journey that returns one to one's Source, will be full of acceptance and the lack of judgment that will be essential for the events that are already beginning to occur.

There are those from other worlds who are preparing to enter the earthplane. There have already been occasional visits, yet this is not yet occurring on a regular basis. It will become an experience that will have to be reconciled within your world. Your world must become prepared to accept those who are engaging in bringing together a universal community. This joining of worlds will be the bringing together of beings from many worlds who are reclaiming their understanding, and preparing for a universal order. Thus the new world order, of which your leaders speak, is only the response of one world to the universal joining of worlds.

You are going through great evolution in your planet. You are moving away from a tribal society to a global society comprised of many cultures. These separations between cultures will begin to break down and become integrated. You will have many new races develop that will be the result of combining those of different color, different nationality, different languages, and different lifestyles. As these relationships emerge, the children born to these relationships will integrate the cultures of the respective families, and the separate races as you now know them will eventually cease to exist. This will be occurring, and has already been occurring, for some time. As these cultures become integrated, as people move to other parts of the world, you will become a world that is of one culture. This culture will contain much diversity, yet will gain the understanding and acceptance that is unable to exist where lines are definitively drawn. Therefore, it will be essential that there be much self-love and self-acceptance for this to occur.

As this is occurring, your technology will continue to advance most rapidly. This will put a great strain on relations among people, which has already begun. Your world will continue to expand its communication until it finds that the management of information will no longer be possible. The breakdown will cause much disturbance, and those who have been most reliant on structure will be filled with much fear.

It is important to begin to base your world on Love. Love will be the foundation on which your world can continue to evolve in a positive direction. Yet, those who are consumed by fear will not be able to make this transition.

It is important when one is on the spiritual path to develop compassion, to be without judgment, and to see with the eye of Love. When one has compassion, one empathizes with the conditions of others, and this empathy gives them understanding of what is needed. This understanding is the basis for mutual support. It is the basis for assisting those not only in your proximity, but around your world, in dealing with the crises that will continue to occur. There will be much upheaval. There will be much fervor in the area of food distribution. There will be great concern about the protection of the environment. Yet Love must prevail, as these crises may also be based upon fear, and fear will not be able to provide positive solutions. Therefore, the evolution of your planet must be based upon the foundation of Love.

Love is accepting. It does not judge another. It accepts the limitations, appearances, and definitions of another. One's own definition, which is their value system, must be respected by others. Therefore, there will be many challenges in your world regarding diversity as your world moves into one integrated culture.

As one learns acceptance of oneself, as one moves that acceptance toward others of the same kind, one must also move that acceptance into all areas. One must accept those of different nationalities, cultures, lifestyles, and also of other worlds. The appearance of those from other worlds will be most curious, frightening for some, and communication will be of a different nature. Thus, as one learns to communicate with those of other cultures, one must also begin to communicate with those who do not communicate with verbal language such as your people do.

One must study the animal kingdom to recognize there are many methods of communication among animals that are not known to man. When one communicates with an animal, one can find a level of communication that appears to be a response to speech, yet one is really communicating by vibrations. These vibrations are positive, accepting, and of positive feeling; or they may be negative and full of fear and anger. Where there is love, the being will advance, will respond to that positive acceptance. Where there is fear, the being will experience rejection and will move away. Therefore, one's communication with these beings will be of acceptance or of fear.

One must learn to be most accepting, yet most discerning. As one encounters beings and languages of other cultures or other worlds, one must be able to sense the vibrations, be aware of the vibrations they emit, and recognize that there is always communication present. The communication may be positive and inviting; it may be negative and rejecting. It is always present.

As your world evolves, it will be essential that your people accept the Invitation to Love and join others on the spiritual path in order to be able to make this transition into a global and a universal community. Those who cannot yet accept will be unable to participate. They will have to return at a later time after much evolution. Therefore, there will be much upheaval on your planet, and this will result in much disturbance between those who are on the spiritual path, and those who are frightened and attacking. As those on the spiritual path move forward, it will be most essential that each be discerning, as there is always rejection and persecution when two major beliefs collide. The collision can be most violent as each feels committed to defending their position. Therefore, it is essential to see with the eye of Love, to see the Higher Self in each being, and to note how that being is made manifest.

As one looks through this bifocal vision, seeing the being as a part of the God-scene, one must also see how that being has been made manifest in the universe. Thus your planet moves ever forward, taking yet another step in its own evolution. These steps, of moving from a tribal culture, to a global culture, to a universal community, will be the essential steps that bring all who would join to unity.

Let your prayers be that you may be accepting of the Invitation to Love, that you may be worthy of the journey, and that you may manifest as a channel for Love and Peace.

May your journey be the result of your God-desire brought to commitment, and moving into Peace. May the Source of your being be that which draws you into the final union. Do not be afraid, for it is that union you most desire.

The New Message of Love
I. Invitation to Love

The New Message of Love
I. Invitation to Love

Love is the Source made manifest. Love is God's presence in your world, and in all worlds. Love is force, action, a magnetic wave drawing all to Itself. Love knows not but Love, yet Love reaches into one's inner being and creates disturbance. Love's mighty force will not allow one to remain complacent. One will be challenged, will be tossed to and fro internally until one makes the choice of whether to accept Love's Invitation.

Love, when it offers the Invitation, is not gentle. Its force interrupts one's life and creates much internal conflict. That conflict must find resolution or one may become ill, begin to act in a different manner, or withdraw. Thus, as the Invitation is given, the channel for Love must be most discerning, as the reaction will be strong.

The invitee will respond by acceptance, by lashing out, by becoming ill, or by withdrawing. Therefore, when the Invitation to Love is extended, the channel must be most cautious. The channel must also be without preference, as preferences may cause disturbance in one's life. If the channel for Love desires that the invitee accept, and this does not occur, the channel may become distraught and go off the spiritual path. Yet the channel may also not discriminate regarding who shall be invited. All are welcome. If the channel is afraid, this fear will become magnified. If the channel has preferences, these, too, will become magnified. Therefore, the channel must be without preference, without fear, and live in the understanding that is available to them.

As Love moves forward, ever touching those who would respond, the response increases. As one makes commitment to Love, one moves forward on one's evolutionary path. One joins all others who are joined, and all move forward. Thus, the one who commits to Love causes much joy in all who are joined. The flock of sheep becomes greater, more dense yet more diverse, as all return to the fold. God is the shepherd, the provider, the protector, and the Source of all. God is great, and Its power is manifest in those who are channels for love.

All who would be channels must accept that there is power and a presence within that is beyond their control. They can only see the result of this power. It is as though the channel were a magnetic field, and as they move forward, that magnetic field draws those who would respond to it. Often the channel is not aware of the presence they carry, yet that presence is made manifest to them so that they may not lose that which they know. It is by understanding this presence that is being carried by the channel for Love, that one can respond to the needs of the invitees. Should they choose to withdraw, the channel must be prepared to let go. Should they become ill, the channel must be prepared to respond as needed. Should they become violent, the channel must be prepared to protect oneself. And should they respond, the channel must be ready to move forward with spiritual support.

The channel for Love must be most diligent in their practice as they carry God into the world. They carry Home, and all that they know. They have understanding to guide them; they have assistance from beyond; and they have the fulfillment that comes with bringing Love into the world.

It is essential to be most focused, to remain frequently with one's Teachers, that all might be prepared. The channel for Love must spend much time in meditation that they may continue to receive. As one receives, one is able to give. Therefore, when one does not receive, one becomes depleted of presence. Presence is always available to those who come into its magnetic field.

Therefore, the channel must always be aware of the reactions of others.

As the channels in your world increase, so they are increasing in other worlds. Thus the magnetic force that is the Source of all continues to move forward, to increase and to fulfill.

As your planet continues its evolution, it will be going through much change. The force that is Love will accelerate this evolution, which is already increasing in speed due to your technology. The technology that you have come to depend upon will not prevail, and there must be other ways of dealing with information that must be discovered.

Your planet is but an infant in much of its development, yet this development will increase rapidly within the next few years. As this evolution proceeds, so does the Invitation to Love increase. Many will become channels. Many will respond adversely. This will create much disturbance within your planet. This disturbance has already begun.

As you move forward to commit to Love, be firm in your decision, be responsive to the call, and find your place in the return to the Source.

Love will provide the direction needed to move through the evolutionary process. It will be the foundation which supports all who would return. Therefore, let none go uninvited.

The New Message of Love
I. Invitation to Love

Chapter Twentyfive

*L*ove is the element that draws all other elements to It. It is a mighty force that pulls all in Its direction that they might join. Love does not enjoin, but invites all to join with It. Therefore, all joining is by choice.

One may choose to join. One may choose to continue with the glitter of the world; yet one is always in charge of one's own choice.

The disruption that will occur in your world will be between those who join, and those who are not yet ready. There will be much dissension; there will be much violence. Yet this evolution cannot be stopped. This evolution is a part of God's Plan for the unification of all worlds. Therefore, one must choose whether to continue with what one already believes, or to step forward and to be open to new understanding through experience.

The experience one will receive will bring them understanding that far surpasses their limited understanding within a belief system. If all belief systems were adequate explanations, they would be in agreement; yet they are full of much disagreement. This disagreement among these systems has created much conflict in your world. There have been wars. There have been persecutions. There have been walls between and among groups. Yet, those who are within belief systems hold firmly in spite of what they know to be true, which is that such different beliefs cannot all be accurate. It is most difficult to step beyond the security of one's belief system and move into experience that is yet unknown.

The one who chooses to move forward into God-experience will have many doubts and concerns, yet will find the experience far surpasses all they could have imagined. They will need to follow each step as it is revealed, to guide them into these experiences. These steps bring one to deeper God-understanding, clarity of direction and decision, safety, security, and understanding. Your people will need to become most disciplined; for they are, at this time, most undisciplined. They treasure their freedom, which is in reality their chaos, and it creates for them much internal conflict. This internal conflict leads to more isolation and away from true relationship. Therefore, one must begin by choosing to follow Love's Invitation to have experience rather than closed belief systems, and to move into that experience one step at a time through disciplined participation.

Love is the Invitation to participate. This participation will bring one to unity with God and all beings. It will fill the emptiness in one's soul that can only be filled by this experience. Therefore, the response to the Invitation to Love is the initiation into experience.

Love draws all toward It. It challenges, unburdens, unites, and moves all forward who would follow. It answers the soul's burning questions: "Why am I here? What am I to do? What is the purpose of my life? Where can I find assistance to resolve these burning questions?" All of these answers begin to come to the one who chooses to respond affirmatively to Love.

Let your heart be open. Let your mind be curious. Let your will be strong that you may be able to respond affirmatively and begin to follow Love. Love has no rewards other than Itself. It fills the empty, brings the lonely to relationship, and quiets one's fears that life has no meaning. Life is full of meaning for those who choose to respond.

The one on the spiritual path who has made the commitment to Experience, to following their understanding, to moving forward with trust, will be most blessed. They will see with new eyes. They will hear with new ears. They will be full to overflowing where once they were empty. Their being will attract others, as Love draws all toward It. They become channels for Love. God's love flows through these channels, ever inviting, and uniting all who would respond. Therefore, those on the spiritual path will be known by the Love that emanates from them, and many will be brought into that Love.

Let your life be a light in the darkness, a channel for Love in a dark and empty world. As your light shines brightly, it renews not only itself, but it brings light to all who will respond. Therefore, darkness is only illuminated by the addition of light. One cannot take away darkness or lack of understanding. One can only bring understanding that it might be accepted or rejected. As the lights burn brightly and generate more light in your world, so this is occurring in all worlds.

Let your light be a beacon to all, that your world might be saved from darkness, and be moved forward into the unification of all worlds.

The New Message of Love
I. Invitation to Love

Praise for **Invitation to Love** by Moriah

During this very disruptive time in our world's history, *Invitation To Love* has arrived "right on time." It's clarity in the midst of chaos. *Invitation To Love* is the calm, clear, yet ever so softly spoken voice we often hear from within ourselves. We feel Its truth, sadly though, we often dismiss it as unheard. At its core, is the message of Love toward ourselves, for one another, and for our Source of All That Is. And, as I took the inner journey into an **Invitation To Love,** I developed a deeper Love [and trust] for this special voice that resides within my Self, *this* same voice within each of us. It was as if *my* inner voice was speaking to me the words my heart already has known for lifetimes. I found **Invitation To Love** as the world's universal guidance system for each of us to return to [the Source] of Love necessary to connect to the purpose of our existence, the evolution of our soul, the unity of our worlds.

The message in an **Invitation To Love** felt familiar to me and I believe you will have a similar experience.

Glenn E. Kakely is author of *Your Power to Create You:*

Discover Your Inner Source of Abundance

Board Certified Hypnotist, Reiki Master,
Natural Wellness Educator-Consultant,
New York.

The New Message of Love
I. Invitation to Love

Moriah is a highly accomplished yet humble Spiritual Master. As I went through her beautiful book, Invitation to Love, the lines seemed to be a Conversation with God...A great teacher is one who knows what the student seeks. The great doctor is one who knows where the pain of the patient resides. A great author is one who knows what the reader needs. However, there is no great teacher, doctor or author who can teach, treat or resolve every issue on this earth. I accurately know now, why *'Invitation to Love'* by Moriah is indeed a 'Sacred Text'.

I am happy to find something fool-proof and handy as an optimum relief for any pain-body, a Midas touch for any disillusioned mind, and a magical healing for any tormented soul.

Asit Ghosh is an accomplished Inspirational Speaker,
Trainer, Behavioral Specialist, Life Coach,
Management Consultant and Author
India.

I was astounded by how many of the words from this sacred text were a reflection of my own journey. *Invitation to Love* offers the reader much truth and wisdom. It is a spiritual road map to our best and highest selves.

Joe Hazen, INHC, is an Integrative

Nutrition Health Coach,

New York.

The New Message of Love
I. Invitation to Love

"What is Love?" has been the question posed by humans since the beginning of time. In her book, Moriah has given us the answer from those closest to its source.. Angelic beings who call themselves the Teachers of Love. Rarely, if ever, have sacred texts for our times been channeled as they have been in this amazing book, Invitation to Love. As one reads, one is reminded that these are the voices of angelic beings speaking to us, and not merely another book about Love. It is indeed an invitation to love emanating from the mind and heart of God, the Source of all to whom we shall all return. That return to Home, as these Teachers of Love refer to it, now has a guidebook in Invitation to Love. These sacred channeled texts are for our Age, for our journey back to Source in these troubled, turbulent times. This invitation to love is not extended to only us on Planet Earth, but to beings throughout the vast Universe. The Teachers of Love have knowledge of other-worldly entities, and seek to have them join with us on our journey back Home to Source from which we all have come.

Diane Hale Smith, Theologian,
Educator, Musician, Photographer;

Co-Founder of Centro Civico

Amsterdam, NY.

Invitation to Love is an insightful guide to a more fulfilling, rewarding life, with God's Love and our Love for each other at the center of our being.

Ruby Dean Collins is author of Mountain Treasures,

West Virginia.

The New Message of Love
I. Invitation to Love

For those who ponder the meaning of life and where things are headed for us individually, as a society, and as a planet, *Invitation To Love* will address it in a richly meaningful, yet simple enough way. This is a book which can be read over and over, and will speak to you at different levels as you move along your path. It brought peace to me in an area of life that I struggled with for many years, simply by showing me that we will all get there. We are helped along, as we help others along, creating a chain of love and connection that moves our planet towards its higher good. Arriving at one's own commitment to a Life of Love will be incredibly rewarding, more so than any other distraction or pleasure of life.

Lisa Nelson, HTCP, is an Author, Musician and
Healing Touch Practitioner
New Jersey.

Spiritual Master Moriah shares pure, genuine wisdom in *Invitation to Love*. This guide to everything, from true, right relationships to opportunities for connection and joining, is insightful and THE way forward for the future.

Janet Tanguay is a Creativity Coach

and owner of Art n Soul, Inc

New York.

Book II.

Journey to Love

Humans often give voice to wanting Love, or God, while giving little priority to this endeavor. Love waits. Love is patient. Love is energy that does not force Itself. Instead, Love waits for the opening, the crack, the voice that welcomes It in. It enters quietly at first. As Its presence is acknowledged, and as the spiritual sojourner desires, It moves into the open and painful places of one's life. It clears chakras, opens minds, challenges old beliefs, encourages action, and begins to move one to more awareness of Its presence.

As this Presence begins to take residence within one's soul, one hungers for more. Hunger and thirst, and the attempt to fill with overindulgence in food and drink, is really the Love-desire. That is also why many on the spiritual path begin to change their diets and daily activities, focusing more on healthy food and beverages, meditation, exercise, and wholeness of mind-body-soul. It is this consciousness of self-care that prepares one for the greater journey of returning to Love. Journey to Love is for the spiritual sojourner who has become more aware of caring for the body as a temple; is accepting of the Invitation to Love; and is ready to take the daily Steps of Journey to Love.

You have come here because of previous preparation. All of this was necessary for you to be able to make the commitment to Love. Surrendering to Love is Step 1, and the most essential step. It is only when you give yourself totally--your desires, ego, need to control, fear--that you are then ready to accept Love as your guide in all decisions.

Love will lead you on a path of greater fulfillment than you could ever achieve in your worldly pursuits. It will calm the aching in your heart. It will bring you to relationships that work to fulfill Spiritual Purpose. It will give meaning and direction. It will cause you to experience deeper love relationships than you thought possible. And it will slowly dissolve your desire for the glitter of the world.

Glitter, through things that tempt you with desire, will lose its hold on your life. You will find new meaning, and new ways to express that meaning. Your heart will be full of love and you will desire to serve according to your Purpose as it is revealed to you. Journey to Love is both a journey and a destination. Be not afraid. Journey to Love is that for which your soul deeply longs. This longing cannot be filled by the world. Attempts to do so will lead to disappointment, failure, loss of faith, illness, and eventually death. Death of understanding is an expensive price to pay to remain isolated.

It is the acceptance of the Invitation to Love, and the subsequent Steps of Journey to Love, that will bring you to Peace.

Journey To Love

"The Preparation"

Journey to Love is the journey to God. It is the spiritual path that takes one from a position of being in the world, to a position of being in the world but not of the world.

The Journey to Love is a journey that is inclusive. All are invited. No one is excluded. The invitation is given to all that all might begin the most wondrous journey Home.

Home is God. Home is where we have come from. Home is that to which we will return. Yet there is much that must be accomplished before we can return Home and remain enjoined. All who return Home are enjoined. They are one. They will never again experience separation. Separation is the return from Home to the earth plane to learn and to contribute one's gifts. One experiences many incarnations until one is ready to join. Thus, all joining occurs until one returns Home.

Many are joining, yet there are many who cannot make the decision to join. They must be lovingly released by those who began the journey to Love. Therefore, the first step in journey to Love is the process of becoming unburdened. All will be left behind that all may be given. That which is no longer essential will be returned to the world. All that is essential will be taken on the journey. Therefore, one may not exist at both levels. As one moves from the level of the world to the level of the spiritual path, one takes a step in one's own evolution and the evolutionary process of the world.

All that is needed will be provided. All that is essential will find inclusion. Yet the step onto the spiritual path is a step of faith as it requires one to release what one has to receive the unknown. Yet the unknown contains all that the heart desires. When one enters the earth plane, one is brought into contact with much that is not essential. Those things of the world that one has been led to believe lead to success do not fulfill the vacuum in the heart. The heart can only be filled with that which it recognizes. Therefore, those things it does not recognize, do not bring fulfillment.

Relationships are brought into proper alignment for the one on the spiritual path. Those relationships that are not essential will fall away. Those which are essential will be brought into one's path. One will need to become most alert, and be prepared to relinquish all that is not in alignment with one's spiritual path. It is a requirement that cannot be understood at the initiation of the journey. Therefore, one must desire God above all. One must return to God through the Journey to Love. The Journey to Love provides all that is essential for the return Home.

As you begin the journey by accepting the invitation to Love, you will meet others who will draw you toward them. They may be supportive of your spiritual journey, or they may tend to pull you off the path. You must be most discerning and committed. You must desire the spiritual path above all. All decisions, all relationships, will be based upon their ability to be supportive of the Journey to Love. You will begin this journey by a decision to commit time to meditation and practice.

This practice is essential to the journey. In other words, one cannot return Home without the journey, and one cannot be on the journey without practice. Therefore, one must accept that one is worthy of the self-discipline essential to devote one's time to meditation and practice.

There will be many obstacles along the journey. There will be many steps that will be most difficult. Yet by relying upon one's inner guidance one may move through all obstacles toward Home. The journey will be most complete. Yet it must be one's priority. One may not say, "I will be here" and go there. In other words, it will require one's full attention and focus.

The one on the spiritual path becomes focused. They carry a Presence which polarizes all with whom they come into contact. Those who desire God will be drawn to them. Those who cannot yet begin the journey will be repelled. Therefore, as one begins the journey, one must begin to be discerning. One must develop communication that is at deeper levels so that one might be protected from those who cannot join until they are ready to receive the invitation.

We will begin by developing discernment and learning true communication. Therefore, we will begin with a lesson on true communication.

Directions: Pages entitled Notes are provided after each lesson for recording insights and experiences. In addition, keeping a private journal is recommended.

The New Message of Love
II. Journey to Love

Lesson #1

Today I will l learn how to truly communicate. True communication is not dependent upon verbal exchange, action or body language. These forms of communication are visible and/or audible. True communication occurs at a level that is neither audible nor visible. It occurs at a vibratory level that draws or repels. It occurs in all life. It is not limited to human and animal forms. It is available for humans, for animals, for the combination, yet it is also available with all that is living. This includes plant life, and it includes humans and other beings who are not of your kind.

As your world evolves, there is much mixing of those of many cultures and languages, and communication is most challenging. Yet true communication exists at levels that do not require verbal, visible, and audible understanding. They occur at a level that is vibratory, and this level will either bring joining, or it will repel those attempting to join into different directions.

As you move into the vicinity of that which is living, you will be drawn, or you will be repelled. There must be no emotion. There must be only acceptance. Acceptance will be that the other is able to join or unable to join. If the other is able to join, you will move forward in your attempts to initiate further communication. However, if the other is unable to join, you must move away as it will be essential for your own protection to do so.

One can practice true communication in all aspects of human endeavor. One can note the reactions that are visible, verbal, and audible, and note whether they are in alignment with the vibratory messages one is receiving. In other words, one may say the right words, yet one may have a distinct feeling that the other is being deceptive.

One may hear the words, "I love you", yet note actions that are not in alignment with the words. One may see one who appears most loving, yet who is unable to say the necessary words because of background and former experience. Therefore, one must begin by developing one's ability to discern whether the messages being received at a vibratory level are consistent or inconsistent with what is occurring in the interaction.

Daily Practice

The lesson for the first week is: in all areas of interaction with others note whether these actions, either verbal, visual, or audible, are in alignment with the vibratory messages one is receiving. This must occur in all interactions throughout the day.

These interactions may be at work, transitions between home and work, at home, during times of entertainment, and during times of intimacy. In other words, all interactions are to be examined for alignment between communication at the level that is verbal, audible, and visible, and the messages at a deeper level that one is receiving. Allow 20 minutes for reflection at the end of each day, and keep a diary of all interactions. Note your response with each interaction. At the end of the day, during the 20-minute practice period, white a short summary of the interactions that occurred.

Complete the activity with a Meditation that begins: "I am open to communication at all levels and I seek that assistance which will enable me to clarify all interactions so that I may learn discernment. I recognize that discernment is essential for the journey to Love, and I willingly accept all that is revealed to me. Thus, I begin the spiritual Journey to Love with the recognition that discernment in communication will assist me to remain on the spiritual path. I will not judge another, yet I will be open to examining each interaction that I may learn and prepare my contribution to the world."

Notes

The New Message of Love
II. Journey to Love

Lesson #2

Communication is a way of joining. It provides the means to bring those who view themselves as separate, together, in the highest level of communication you call intimacy.

There is a union of self so that two become one. Intimacy is more than physical joining. The purest level of intimacy is joining at the levels of mental, emotional, physical, and spiritual. When that occurs simultaneously, there is union that is like the joining of one with God.

Joining is the greatest desire one has. All of life on the earth plane is an attempt to join. The joining of lovers, or parent and child, contain all four levels of joining. Other relationships generally contain at most three, as all cannot physically join. Yet there can be joining by touch, by birth, by sexuality.

This complete joining is a union that all desire, yet the romance in your culture leads to joining that is incomplete. It relies upon physical and emotional joining. It sometimes includes mental joining, yet there is not an emphasis on spiritual joining.

Spiritual joining is more than religious joining. In your world, people frequently join because they are, as they say, of a similar faith or religion. Yet this is not true spiritual joining though it may include spiritual joining. In other words, spiritual joining is much more than a tendency toward similar belief patterns. In order to unite spiritually, each must be on a spiritual path, moving in concert with the other. In other words, they must work at spiritual practice, and they must be able to respond to spiritual experience.

They must be able to support one another's growth and they must be able to serve as validators for one another. In other words, joining spiritually is not stagnant. It is movement along two individual paths that are joined.

True intimacy occurs when there is joining at every level. This is the highest level of intimacy. Though there are other levels that may also be enjoyed, they will not provide the fulfillment each is seeking. When you find true intimacy, you are married already. In other words, the marriage already existed. One does not choose marriage; one discovers marriage. And once marriage is discovered, one will not be able to find fulfillment with another.

When true intimacy is discovered, it creates much disruption in the lives of those who have discovered it together as they are often in other relationships. This creates much pain and guilt as they are not able to understand why they must leave their current relationship for another. Yet when one discovers marriage by experiencing true intimacy, one cannot return to the previous stage without much pain and suffering. One must leave one's former life behind to join the one with whom one was previously committed. True marriage begins before entrance to life on the earth plane.

Daily Practice

Consider for one week your current relationships. Determine if you are joined spiritually, mentally, emotionally, physically. Look without judgment at your primary relationships to discover the level of intimacy you experience. Write about each level in each relationship. Be honest and share this with no one who could be injured by the sharing. In other words, find another who can be most objective and understanding, and who can maintain confidentiality. Consider whether your primary relationship supports your spiritual practice and provides the intimacy essential for your evolution so that you may contribute your gifts to the world.

Begin your 20-minute meditation with the affirmation: "I acknowledge my evolution beyond the earth plane. I acknowledge that I have entered the earth plane to learn and to contribute. I acknowledge my desire for true intimacy."

The New Message of Love
II. Journey to Love

Notes

Lesson #3

Communication is the means of relationship between two or more beings. This communication may be verbal, action, body language, and vibrational. It can occur at any one level or at many levels simultaneously. It can move from one level to multiple levels and continue that movement back and forth. In other words, it is not fixed.

As you encounter others, it is important to learn the communication needs and to begin to understand each communication level and combination of levels. Each may mean different things in different circumstances, and these circumstances may be cultural means of communication used by that society and may also reflect the origin of that particular being. In other words, communication is a means of relating between two or more like or unlike beings. This can become most confusing when one considers the many variables, yet it is at the vibrational level that most communication occurs.

Communication at the vibrational level is found between and among human beings, animals, plants, and any combination of these. It also occurs in those instances when one encounters beings of other realities and other worlds. It is through the vibrations of thoughts and emotions that true communication occurs.

As one begins to study this intricate system, we call communication, one must begin to learn in small segments. It can be most overwhelming to try to deal with communication in a broad sense without considering the parts. Therefore, we will begin practice by considering, for the period of one week, verbal communication between two or more human beings.

Daily Practice

For one week, at the end of each day, write down the names of all with whom you had verbal communication. You may also consider keeping a list throughout the day as this may assure that there are no omissions. However, do not comment on any of the communications until you begin a reflective period of 30 minutes to review the communications of the day. Look for similarities. Look for differences. Consider whether or not you were speaking on the phone, or you were receiving simultaneous body language by being present with the person or persons.

> What was the emotional tone?
> Did it change throughout the conversation?
> What did you feel was really being said?
> What was the tone of the communication?
> Did it invite you to communicate again, or did it tend to close off possibility of future communication?
> Was it a communication that was complete in itself or did it require follow-up?
> Was it with a friend, or one you did not know?

Consider these and many more variables, and look for underlying information that was not spoken yet which you acquired. Make notes about the communication, and note how much communication occurs without words.

Begin your 20-minute meditation with the following affirmation:

"I am a student of true communication. I desire to know the beings with whom I am relating. I am learning to communicate what I truly desire

to communicate by learning to understand communication from others. I will learn true communication so that I can truly join."

Lesson #4

Communication is love made manifest. Love cannot exist where there is no communication at any level. Therefore, the desire to join is made possible through communication, and communication allows one to accept the invitation to join.

Communication brings together those with much familiarity, with some or little familiarity, and with no familiarity. In other words, communication is the bridge that joins from the initiation of relationship through profound relationship should that occur. Communication provides the context for joining. Yet that communication may be made manifest in many ways.

We will begin by considering communication that is verbal. This communication may be with those of comparable language development in the same language, within a similar language yet of different levels of ability to use the language, and it may be between those of different languages where there may be no understanding of the other language, or some understanding. The communication is on a verbal level and utilizes a language as the vehicle for joining.

When two people speak the same language, they use many words that have a variety of meanings, and there may be confusion as to the meaning being assigned to the word. In others words, language is made up of symbols you call words, and these symbols may represent one thing for one person and something different for another. Therefore, even between those of comparable ability in the use of a common language, there may be misunderstanding due to the meaning associated with each word. Two people may speak to one another, and each may think that they have communicated adequately, yet the message received may have a different interpretation. Therefore, what has been the intended communication has not been received.

Daily Practice

We will begin to study communication between two of comparable ability of a common language. For a period of one week, list the people with whom you have verbal communication, and at the end of each day, review those communications:

> Were they complete?
> Do you feel that what you tried to communicate was received?
> Were you careful to present the information in more than one way to allow for understanding?
> Did you check for understanding by asking the other for their understanding of what you said?

In this lesson it will be important to begin to understand whether what you are attempting to communicate is in fact that which is received. Begin your 20-minute meditation with the following affirmation:

"I desire to communicate with others as a vehicle for joining. I recognize the importance of expressing my thoughts in ways that can be understood by another. I will check for understanding and will be willing

to change my way of expressing to meet the needs of the one who is receiving my communication. I will be willing to use a variety of opportunities and strategies to ensure that the message has been accurately received. I understand that it is my responsibility to express my thoughts in a way that can be accurately received."

Complete the meditation with this affirmation: *"I am open to communication at all levels, and I seek that assistance which will enable me to clarify all interactions so that I may learn discernment. I recognize that discernment is essential for the journey to Love, and I willingly accept all that is revealed to me. Thus, I begin the spiritual journey to Love with the recognition that discernment in communication will assist me to remain on the spiritual path. I will not judge another, yet I will be open to examining each interaction that I may learn and prepare my contribution to the world."*

The New Message of Love
II. Journey to Love

Notes

Lesson #5

Communication that is received from another is open to many interpretations. These interpretations may be based upon ability to communicate within the language. Therefore, when one uses words that are unknown to another, clarification as to meaning is required. It is also true that words that are used even most commonly carry many different meanings, and these meanings also are each open to interpretation. Therefore, there are many opportunities for inaccuracy and incompleteness. It is essential to check for understanding for another's communication. When you receive a communication, it is most important to rephrase that information to ascertain whether you have correctly interpreted what you have received.

Daily Practice

During the day note everyone with whom you speak. At the close of the day, review each interaction:

Did you repeat the information you received in at least one other way to check for accuracy?

Did you ask for clarification when the meaning received was not the same as what was intended?

Did you continue to seek clarification until a common understanding was reached?

Did you have a feeling of unity with the other at the moment that true understanding was achieved?

What were your feelings at the moment of understanding in each verbal transaction?

Begin your 20-minute meditation with the following affirmation:

"It is my responsibility to check for understanding for any communication that I receive. I will seek to fully understand the other, even though I may not agree with their opinion. I recognize that in relationship, understanding of position is of more importance than agreement. Therefore, I will ensure that in every verbal transaction, I understand what is being communicated. I will indicate that understanding though I need not indicate agreement. It is this understanding rather than agreement that provides unity."

The New Message of Love
II. Journey to Love

The New Message of Love
II. Journey to Love

Notes

Lesson #6

Communication is that which will bring all to God. Not all who communicate will return, yet those who choose to return do so through communication. Therefore, communication is the vehicle for this returning to occur.

There are many occurrences in your world that will require you to be calm, and capable, in the area of communication. These occurrences include the movement of your people resulting in the mixing of many cultures; the economic interdependence, which is becoming more apparent to you; and the societal changes requiring the combination of resources of many of your institutions. In other words, those areas that formerly allowed separation and independence, will now require interdependence.

There are other changes that are occurring simultaneously. You are being visited by not of this Earth. While intelligence is understandable to you, the lifestyles and ways of existing and surviving are unknown to your people. Therefore, as these Beings who are more highly developed, and therefore able to more easily travel to your planet, increase their visitations, there will be occurrences where there will be a mixing of Beings of different planets. This mixing will require communication, yet it cannot rely on communication as you have known.

The communication that will be essential for understanding another of another planet will require that you be able to communicate on all levels. That is why you are beginning a curriculum in communication. We have been working with you as you study communication between two of a similar language with comparable ability and without comparable ability within this language. Yet you will need to begin to be aware of communication on all levels. There is also much variation within each level.

Daily Practice

We will continue our study by noting facial expressions in those verbal transactions of two of common language. This will include those of comparable verbal ability, and those who are not of comparable ability. In other words, it is important to begin to note facial expressions in all transactions when one can be seen by another. During the day, note all verbal transactions that occur when you could see one another. At the end of the day, review transactions, noting facial expressions.

Did the expression seem consistent with the message you were receiving?

Did the expression seem to convey a different message from the one you were receiving?

Was there enthusiasm? Was there apathy? Was there pain? Was there delight?

Was the other trying to convince you to join in his or her view point?

Note this and many other possible reactions. As you move through the weekly lesson, note whether you are becoming more aware of the facial expressions of the other at the time of the transaction. Begin to note whether the facial expression is consistent with the message, or appears to be giving a different message. If so, what is the other message?

Begin your 20-minute meditation with the following affirmation:

"I seek to know and respond to every communication. I desire to know the true meaning of the communication, and then become open to what is occurring on other levels. I will listen with both my ears and my eyes as well as my feelings to be able to respond to the communication that is really occurring. I desire to emanate love through communication, and this can best be done by developing communication that can hear and respond to all levels. Therefore, I commit myself to the study of true communication that I might be able to facilitate the changes that are occurring. My service to God, or Love, will be through the development of true communication."

The New Message of Love
II. Journey to Love

Notes

Questions for Reflection

1. Who are the people who support my spiritual journey?

2. From whom can I receive more support?

3. What do I need to feel supported?

4. Who or what is blocking my support?

The New Message of Love
II. Journey to Love

5. If I could have the ideal situation to evolve spiritually, what would it be like?

6. Describe the best experience I have had that supported me mentally, emotionally, physically, and spiritually.

The New Message of Love
II. Journey to Love

The New Message of Love
II. Journey to Love

Notes

JOURNEY TO LOVE

"THE JOURNEY"

In our deepest times, faith is challenged. Words and songs of religious life may appear shallow in the face of fear of death. Your people live by faith. They have often designed their worship time to be preacher/teacher-centered. While some wisdom may be shared, it is the heart of the individual person that opens, or closes, to Love.

When you came to earth, you still retained some memory of that time between lives you call heaven. As you moved forward into your daily experience of the world, new memories developed, and old memories before life on earth faded. They are lost or forgotten now, but will return upon your return! In other words, when you return Home, you remember Home, and your worldly memories fade. What remains of life on earth is connections which continue until your next assignment. At that point, your earthly assignment is complete, and you are free to remember and reconnect with loved ones.

It is true that the coming and going of souls from one assignment to another causes feelings of loss as ones' missions now briefly diverge. One continues his/her mission on earth, while the other moves forward to reflect, remember, renew, and move to one's next lessons. Thus, the lessons of life are but a few at a time, each within a new assignment.

Each lesson builds upon previous learning. Thus, the one on a spiritual path continues the Journey to Love.

You are a channel of Love and Peace through eternity, but first you must Love. The Journey to Love begins here. You are ready. It is now time.

Note:

The Steps in Journey to Love are given here as received in order to retain authenticity. It is important not to be turned off toward the authoritative tone, but to recognize that the Guidance given is the path for your journey. At times the language may seem awkward. This sacred text is delivered as received for your highest benefit.

Directions:

Each Step is to be done daily for one week. You will note that some of the Steps suggest writing your responses. You may choose to record verbally rather than write if that is your preference. It is important to record in such a way that responses are always available for your review. A blank page for notes is included for convenience and easy reference. It is suggested that you find a special time and place for your daily meditative Step. A quiet place, adequate soft lighting, and items that are meaningful and enjoyable to you can support your experience. It is also important to keep your notes or recorder easily accessible to capture ideas as they come to you.

As you move forward with Steps, you may begin to notice a sense or feeling of energy or Presence. Your Meditations may become a place where much becomes known to you. The Spiritual Path is full of Experience. Experience takes you more deeply into intuitive knowing and understanding. As you progress you will move beyond simply faith, to knowing through Experience. The **Journey to Love** is a deepening of spiritual experience, guidance, direction, fulfillment, and peace.

WEEK 1　　　　　　　　　　　　　　　STEP 1

This Step is to be done daily for one week.

Open your heart to accept Love. Ask in prayer that Love come into your soul and bring you fulfillment and peace. Say in prayer that you are ready to begin a new life in Love with these words:

"I surrender myself to Love. I ask that Love guide me in all decisions. I ask for strength to detach from my former desires that were unhealthy and not fitting for my Path. I ask that those relationships that support my Journey become apparent, and that those unable to support me fall away. I release them with love. Make me Your person in the world that I might serve in the ways that I am uniquely designed to serve. Make me a Channel of Your Love and Peace through eternity."

The New Message of Love
II. Journey to Love

Notes

WEEK 2   STEP 2

Now that you have surrendered to Love, asked for Guidance in all decisions, and made the commitment to follow Love in all your life, it is time to evaluate your current situation. Take a sheet of paper and divide into 2 columns. Column one is a list of those people who will support your new Journey. Column 2 is a list of those people who are unable at this time to support you.

After reviewing each list, place the paper out of sight. Meditate daily with the following prayer:

"These people who are my friends may or may not be able to support me in my new Journey. I recognize that to be strong, I will require support. Now let those who can support, come forward. Allow those who are unable, to fall away. Support me through this challenging time, that I might not resist, but that I may be able to release with love all who are unable to support my journey. Let everything I do be done for Love."

The New Message of Love
II. Journey to Love

Notes

The New Message of Love
II. Journey to Love

WEEK 3   STEP 3

Over time those who can support the one on the Spiritual Path will move into prominence, while those who cannot make the Journey will begin to fall away. Assess your interactions during the past 7 days. Reflect upon any persons who have moved forward in support. Acknowledge those who have experienced difficulty moving forward with you. How do you know that those who appear to support you are truly able to commit to that assignment? How do you know those who are unable to support you? What evidence do you see? At this time you may see someone unexpectedly come forward in support. You may also note that there are others moving away. Allow this to occur without resisting.

Each day after reflection, pray:

"Help me to accept that not everyone will be able to support me. May I not attempt to convince nor sway them. Instead, may I accept their decision with love. I recognize that as my vibration shifts, those who are pulled toward that vibration will also shift. It is a spiritual truth that vibrations attract other like vibrations. Those who cannot engage or accept this increased energy will fall away. Help me to resist the desire to control. Help me to accept that all is going according to the Plan."

The New Message of Love
II. Journey to Love

Notes

The New Message of Love
II. Journey to Love

WEEK 4   STEP 4

You are now beginning to note a shift in what holds your interest. You desire stillness and peace, and long to avoid disruption and drama. Those relationships that are unable to support you are falling away. Whether by a gentle drift, or a fiery angry split, the ability to move forward on the Spiritual Path has taken precedence. You may feel a longing for old relationships. Resist the urge to run after those that have moved away. See who comes forward. When you are consciously on the spiritual Journey to Love, you are never alone. When in meditation, daily, ask for the following:

"The path is sometimes lonely and I may feel afraid. Yet, I acknowledge that I am never alone, for Love is always with me. Love is an energy that pervades all. It holds one close when afraid, holds one up when challenged, holds one back when angry. Love heals old wounds, and takes up residence where wounds once were. Let Love be my Guide in all decisions."

(A page for your notes has been added for your convenience. You will also need a notebook and pen for all of the following Steps. A recording device may be substituted as long as all previous responses can be easily located and reviewed.)

Notes

WEEK 5   STEP 5

Spiritual purpose is beginning to emerge. As you release old desires for the glitter of the world--social life, ambition, competition, status--in favor of personal time for reflection, new issues and desires will emerge. Dreams of long ago may arise. Memories of past interests may again begin to come to the fore. Certain people, activities, or publications may trigger unexplained desires for creativity. A need to express through art, music, writing, or other art form may surface. Follow these desires to again express that which has long been repressed. Do not judge these impulses. Simply follow, and note whether they hold any purpose in this new life.

Each day in meditation, with pen and notebook (or audio recorder) beside you, ask:

"What do You want me to do?" After a brief reflection, write anything that first comes to mind.

The New Message of Love
II. Journey to Love

Notes

WEEK 6   STEP 6

Review what you have written on each of the past 7 days. Note any repetition, if it exists. From where do you think each idea originates? Write what you feel each response means. Each day in meditation, ask:

"Why am I here? What do You want me to do? I know that my life has Purpose, and I desire to fulfill that Purpose. Please reveal to me that which remained hidden in my past, so that I may bring forth my Purpose in the world. I know that I am uniquely designed to serve."

Each day, write, without judgment, any thoughts that come to you.

The New Message of Love
II. Journey to Love

Notes

WEEK 7   STEP 7

Review all of your written or recorded responses. Ask, "What am I to learn from this?" Write whatever first comes to mind. Repeat daily for one week.

In meditation each day, pray: *"Help me to understand my Purpose. Guide me as I reflect and write. Help me to hear internally. Lead the way that I might follow. 'Make me an instrument of Your peace."*

The New Message of Love
II. Journey to Love

Notes

WEEK 8   STEP 8

By now you are noting that some of your friends have moved away. Others have come forward. New people have arrived in your life. Some friends will take interest in your thoughts. Others will feel that you have become "too serious." Still others will appear to withdraw, or question your actions. This is a natural part of spiritual awakening and commitment. All that is not necessary will fall away. All that is needed will be provided.

In meditation daily, reflect upon those few with whom you feel close, even if they are new friends. Ask that your relationships that support your Spiritual Purpose become more pronounced, and that those who are unable to support you may be released with love. Ask that you be able to release all--people, activities, and material items--that you might move forward on your path.

The New Message of Love
II. Journey to Love

Notes

WEEK 9   STEP 9

As you move more deeply into your spiritual practice, Journey to Love, you may begin to question, "What will I be asked to do? What will I be asked to give up? Who will I need to release?" This is a somewhat painful, sometimes euphoric time. Emotions may run from depression to anger, to sadness, to joy. It is a time of spiritual cleansing. As you relinquish all that cannot go with you on this Path, recognize that you are never alone. Your Teacher Guides go before you, to prepare your way. They assist you when you are weak. They rejoice with you at each Step accomplished.

In Meditation each day, pray:

"I am never alone. The Teachers of Love prepare, guide and assist me at all times. I will always have the strength to do the Steps if I first call upon Them. I will begin each Meditation with the words, 'The Teachers of Love are with me.'"

The New Message of Love
II. Journey to Love

Notes

WEEK 10   STEP 10

Some days you may feel deeply committed to following your Spiritual Path. Other days you may become distracted with the activities and demands of daily life. Select a symbol that will be your reminder that you are never alone, and that the Teachers of Love are with you. Place that symbol in a variety of places as a reminder. This will help you to increase your awareness at all times of day of your spiritual journey.

In each daily meditation, set the intention to be consciously on your Spiritual Path at all times. Say, *"I intend to be constantly consciously aware of my spiritual commitment, and my spiritual journey, including all that will be revealed."*

Notes

WEEK 11   STEP 11

Spiritual experience is direct personal experience of a unique event. This may include feeling, knowing, seeing, hearing, touching, and other little-understood intuitive events. Each person has unique gifts which only truly emerge after commitment and practice. These events are not to be feared, but to be accepted as part of the unfolding of spiritual understanding.

In each daily Meditation, ask that what is needed be provided. Ask to increase your capacity to accept spiritual experience.

Say: "I am open to spiritual experience and the lessons that will be provided. I call upon the Teachers of Love for protection, guidance, and understanding."

The New Message of Love
II. Journey to Love

Notes

WEEK 12   STEP 12

Reflect upon any unusual experiences you may have had. These are experiences that others may attempt to explain away, but for which there appears to be no rational answer. Write down each unexplained event, and note your age, reaction, and what it meant to you. Each day, as you reflect, remember when others' attempts to "explain away" this event caused you to deny or forget the experience.

In each daily Meditation, ask for those unexplained life events to come forward in your consciousness to be written down, and reflected upon.

Say, *"Thank You for this life I have been given. Thank you for events that have brought me to this place on my Journey. Reveal to me those events that I may have forgotten, but which influence my direction. Help me not to be afraid, but to open to new possibilities."*

The New Message of Love
II. Journey to Love

Notes

WEEK 13 — STEP 13

Each day, begin to meditate for a few minutes. Stop meditating, and write down any thoughts that come to you. Do not judge your thoughts as they arise. Simply write, and do not stop the flow.

In Meditation, say:

"I ask for the Teachers of Love to be with me now, and at all times. I ask for whatever I need to know to be revealed to me as I write. I give thanks for this Guidance. I will work to understand more each day."

The New Message of Love
II. Journey to Love

Notes

WEEK 14 — STEP 14

Journey to Love is the guidance from the Teachers of Love to bring each person into union with Love. Love is God. Love is Higher-Power. Love is the Source. Love is energy in all Beings. As you do each Step with deep desire and devotion, you will be brought closer to that complete union. Allow nothing to keep you from Love. Love heals. Love guides. Love moves you forward toward your unique Purpose in the world.

In Meditation each day, ask:

"Take away anything that would take me off my Spiritual Path. Make the way clear. Hold me in Love. Guide my steps daily. 'Make me an instrument of Your Peace.'"

The New Message of Love
II. Journey to Love

Notes

WEEK 15   STEP 15

As you proceed on your Spiritual Journey, see who can support you. Who can help you? Who understands? Who cares? Make a list of those people with whom you can share your true desires and dreams.

In daily Meditation, ask the following:

"What do You want me to do? Who can help me?" Write your responses as they come to you. At the end of the Meditation, review what you have written.

Notes

The New Message of Love
II. Journey to Love

WEEK 16   STEP 16

Finding a time and a place where you are not distracted is essential for the Spiritual Sojourner. Where can you be alone with your thoughts? Consider where you can go at least once per week for a few hours of silence. Here you might write, meditate, paint, draw, walk, or find solace. Here you will be able to hear the inspiration that comes to you. Lack of distraction from people and events is essential for the Spiritual Sojourner to continue to advance. Make a list of those places where you can be alone with your thoughts and expressions without distraction.

In Meditation each day, say: "Thank You for the spiritual awareness to which I have opened. I am aware that I need time alone to be able to continue to grow. Guide me to where I can find opportunity for spiritual experience and expression. 'Let all I do be done for Love.' "

The New Message of Love
II. Journey to Love

Notes

WEEK 17   STEP 17

You are now aware of places, environments, where you can be alone with your thoughts. Keep a notebook to record your thoughts and insights at all times. When you go to bed, keep your pen and notebook beside you to record dreams, experiences, inspiration, or new awareness. This is the true beginning of a lifelong interaction with Love through your Teachers. You will need to always have a way to record inspiration as it comes to you. Now that you are becoming open, that inspiration may come to you at all times and spaces as long as you remain open to listening internally.

In Meditation, say:

"Thank You that I am growing in spiritual experience and my ability to receive guidance. I know that this will continue as long as I remain open to receive. Help me to stay on my Path, and follow my Steps daily. Thank You for all that has been revealed, and all that is about to be revealed to me."

The New Message of Love
II. Journey to Love

Notes

The New Message of Love
II. Journey to Love

WEEK 18   STEP 18

Spiritual growth and development are much like growth and development of a child. If nurtured daily, it will grow and develop in positive ways. If neglected, it will fall into difficulty. It is time to make a life commitment to follow Spiritual Purpose where it leads. This is a divine moment. Choose something that will be symbolic of this commitment that you will keep with you daily. Some people have chosen a ring, symbolizing their commitment to Love.

In Meditation daily, ask that an appropriate and special way to reflect the commitment you are about to make be revealed to you. Say, *"As I prepare to make a spiritual commitment of my life to follow Love where It leads, I ask that ideas of an object that symbolizes my commitment be revealed to me. Guide me always that I may be your instrument of peace and love."*

The New Message of Love
II. Journey to Love

Notes

WEEK 19   STEP 19

Review all of your writings to date. Notice any repetitious words or phrases. Write these down. Make a list of all thoughts that seem to be especially relevant to you on your Path.

In daily Meditation, say: *"Thank You for the words and ideas given to me. Help me to remember, understand, and grow into what You have uniquely designed for me."*

The New Message of Love
II. Journey to Love

Notes

WEEK 20 STEP 20

Some of your friends are less attentive. Some may have dropped away. Your primary relationships are those that can support you, or take you off your Path. Note especially your spouse, significant other, boyfriend or girlfriend, or best friend. This relationship is the one most likely to support you, or keep you from following your path. Examine closely this primary relationship. Make a list of those qualities you like, and those you find difficult to accept. Ask of each characteristic, "Why do I like this? Why does this quality make me uncomfortable?" Note any qualities you may find unacceptable.

In Meditation, say, *"I desire to stay on my Spiritual Path. I recognize that I will require relationships that support me. I ask that only those relationships that can support me flourish, and those that would take me off my path, fall away. I ask for strength to help me through this process."*

The New Message of Love
II. Journey to Love

Notes

WEEK 21   STEP 21

As your relationships shift, new areas of disagreement may appear. Step back objectively and ask yourself, "Is this disagreement of importance to me? Is it a symptom of our pulling away?"

In Meditation, ask that what is necessary to this relationship be revealed to you as needed.

The New Message of Love
II. Journey to Love

Notes

WEEK 22 — STEP 22

Grief is a product of loss. When those people who may have been right for us are no longer able to support us, this can be one of life's most painful experiences. Holding on to that which no longer serves our needs spiritually can take us off our Path. Releasing with Love can help us through this step. Although the other may react in pain and lashing out, you can find comfort in the peaceful acknowledgement that it is time to move forward alone on your Spiritual Path while remembering that you are never alone.

In Meditation daily, ask: *"What do You want me to do? Give me strength to move forward alone, in the knowledge that I am never alone."*

The New Message of Love
II. Journey to Love

Notes

WEEK 23 STEP 23

Develop the habit of Presence. This is to cultivate the conscious awareness that you are constantly in the Presence of Love. Love is not something to be called upon only at special occasions or even relegated only to daily meditation and prayer. Practice several times daily with the thought, "And every word a prayer." This is the consciousness of constant Presence.

In Meditation daily, say: *"I desire to live daily in the Love consciousness. Make every thought, interaction, word, a prayer that Love is with us and guides us. We are never alone."*

The New Message of Love
II. Journey to Love

Notes

WEEK 24   STEP 24

You are now realizing that Presence is with you with thought. You may feel or sense Presence when you think of Love, or Teachers of Love. There is an invisible connection between thought and Presence. Therefore, only you can deny the presence of Presence. Love is not pushy. It comes in when invited. It becomes a more constant awareness with practice. As you continue your daily Meditations through Journey to Love, this Presence will make Itself more apparent to you. Only you decide your Path, and only you can make the decision for lifelong commitment.

Meditate daily, asking that Presence be present with you. Ask to be able to sense Presence, and to be reassured that Love is always with you.

The New Message of Love
II. Journey to Love

Notes

WEEK 25   STEP 25

You are learning not only to call upon, but to call in Presence, or Love. This is a result of continuous meditative practice and deep desire for Love. Love knows your heart. Love fills a vacuum in the heart that nothing but Love can fill. Begin each daily Meditation activity by asking Love to be present with you. This can be done silently, internally. This is inviting the constant presence of Presence.

In daily Meditation, give thanks for the Invitation to Love. Acknowledge your deep desire to continue to grow in spirit and in truth.

The New Message of Love
II. Journey to Love

Notes

WEEK 26   STEP 26

Progressing on the spiritual path may take many twists and turns, yet the Path can serve to steady and center you. Since you began this Path, what events have occurred in these 26 weeks? How did you react to each? Is your reaction different from what it used to be, or would probably have been? Write and reflect upon each, including any that may be occurring at this time.

In daily Meditation, ask to become centered and react from a place of Peace. Say, *"In all things and at all times, may I be an instrument of Peace."*

Notes

WEEK 27   STEP 27

"You are a channel of Peace and Love through eternity..." This is that to which a spiritual sojourner aspires. Bringing peace and love to worldly pain and suffering is our mission and deepest desire. People go through periods of personal and family loss, accidents, and illness. These are among the greatest of human challenges. Bringing peace to suffering is how the spiritual sojourner enhances quality of life for others. This service may take many forms, but the essence is the same.

Consider where you are drawn to serve. What were your dreams? Did they become forgotten in everyday stressors? List those dreams you once had. Do not judge them to be inappropriate or silly. Within those dreams may be a truth of who you will become. Make lists. Reflect. Write anything that comes to you

In Meditation ask to know: *"What would You have me do? What is my Purpose in the world?"*

The New Message of Love
II. Journey to Love

Notes

The New Message of Love
II. Journey to Love

WEEK 28   STEP 28

Your life on the spiritual path is more like a puzzle than a strategic plan. You are designed to follow, rather than create, the Plan for your life. The Plan already exists. Through spiritual practice, meditation, prayer, practicing constant Presence, you receive each step only after the previous step is complete. Some steps take longer if the lesson requires more time to be learned. Therefore, your progression depends upon completing a step on your path, and understanding the lesson of that step.

In Business, you may have been asked to develop a 5-year, or long-term plan, and steps to achieve that plan. On the spiritual path, you complete your current step, and the next one is revealed to you.

In daily Meditation, ask the Teachers of Love: *"What is my next step?"* Write down all insights as they were received.

The New Message of Love
II. Journey to Love

Notes

WEEK 29   STEP 29

Letting go is one of the challenging lessons that is repeated frequently on the spiritual path. At any moment you may be attempting to let go of an idea, material object, lifestyle, location, relationship, child, money, fear, control. Notice those things and ideas you find most difficult to release. That may give you an idea of where you are inappropriately attached. Inappropriate attachments may limit your progress on the Spiritual Path. List any areas where you feel you need to work toward releasing.

In Meditation each day, say, *"I am eager to progress on my Spiritual Path. Reveal to me the areas where I need to practice release."*

Write down those areas, and any thoughts that occur with them. Reflect and Meditate upon them during the week, adding others as necessary, and eliminating those that no longer control you.

The New Message of Love
II. Journey to Love

Notes

WEEK 30   STEP 30

Trust is most important on the Spiritual Path. Often trust is given that is not deserved, and there are many negative consequences to the spiritual sojourner. Consider past relationships where you trusted, and then were betrayed or had your trust abused. List those people. Consider them individually. What was your gut telling you about that person before you trusted? What was your gut telling you about the relationship? Your intuition, or gut reaction, contains more information than you mentally process. While you may have assessed that this person was trustworthy, your gut may have been giving you important information that you ignored. With each name, consider if you would have trusted them had you listened to your gut reaction.

In Meditation each day, ask to develop your profound intuition, or instinctual response. Say, *"Help me to grow in awareness of my instinctual response, my profound intuition. Help me to trust this intuition, and always compare it with my intellectual assessment in order to know who is worthy of my trust."* Note any changes you are able to make during the week with this new awareness.

The New Message of Love
II. Journey to Love

Notes

WEEK 31   STEP 31

Review your writings. What new awareness have you gained? What are repeated themes? Note all new awareness. Write down your questions regarding these lessons. List these questions in the order they feel most compelling.

In daily Meditation, say, *"Thank You for new insights I have gained through Journey to Love. As I review each remaining question I have listed, I will listen for Your response."*

Continue this practice by meditating for 1-2 minutes after reviewing a question. Quickly write whatever comes to mind. When the flow of the response stops or lessens, continue with the next question by meditating 1-2 minutes, and then writing the response,

The New Message of Love
II. Journey to Love

Notes

WEEK 32 STEP 32

Review your writing from Step 31. As you read, more questions may emerge. Write each question down for further clarification. Meditate and then write the response to each question. If your responses were complete and you have no further questions, ask another question that is on your mind. Write the response. Throughout the week, write any questions that come to you, and meditate about each, followed by writing the response you receive.

Each day in Meditation, express gratitude for this wondrous way of questioning and receiving a response. Give gratitude that you now know that you are never alone.

The New Message of Love
II. Journey to Love

Notes

WEEK 33   STEP 33

A challenging but essential practice with channeled responses is to check that response against your gut instinct. Did it feel right? Did you feel that the response was independent of the answer you desired? Your fears and your preferences can influence and impact the answers you believe you are receiving. Therefore, it is essential for you to center yourself, and ask to be in a space of no fear and no preference. It is only when you have arrived, through meditation and practice, at being without fear or preference regarding the question or issue upon which you are focusing, that you may accept the answer as a true response.

In Meditation, ask (always) for the Teachers of Love to be present and guide you. Ask to be in a state without fear or preference. When you feel that centered space of equilibrium, then focus on the question and receive the response. Check the response against your gut, your intuitive instinct. Does this response feel right?

Use this process daily to gain spiritual guidance in all areas of your life.

The New Message of Love
II. Journey to Love

Notes

WEEK 34   STEP 34

Your world is full of much diversity. As travel and mobility have increased, you may interact with many people of other cultures, and languages. It is not practical to learn every language, but it is essential to be able to communicate. Therefore, you will need ways other than words to communicate. This area of development is known as telepathy. It is not so much about reading others' thoughts, though some will become skilled enough to do so. However, it is essential to be able to acknowledge another's intentions, and to be able to acknowledge with confidence these intentions within yourself.

Every day for one week, note each person with whom you come into contact. Write down any information you gained about each that you learned without language. Did you notice their clothing? Did it give you ideas about their work or hobbies? Did they have distinctive characteristics? Did they wear clothing or jewelry that showed affiliation to marriage, organization, or philosophy? Did they have a regional accent? List everything that you noticed without communication through words or language.

In daily Meditation, ask to become more aware of others' intentions. Ask to increase your ability to sense information intuitively. Give thanks for all of your new awareness gained through Journey to Love.

The New Message of Love
II. Journey to Love

Notes

WEEK 35 STEP 35

Consider all of the people you interacted with last week, and others that you met this week. These meetings do not require formal introductions. It could be at your school, community organization, place of worship, or place of business. With each interaction from these two weeks, consider, "Did I feel safe with that person? What characteristics did I note beyond what was learned through language?" List each person and what you learned about each beyond words.

In Meditation each day, ask to increase your awareness regarding others true motives. Ask for protection through following your instinct and intuition. Ask for protection from any Other who might intend to harm you.

The New Message of Love
II. Journey to Love

Notes

WEEK 36   STEP 36

In Meditation we reach for the Beyond. We seek connection, protection, guidance, and reassurance that we are not alone. It is essential to understand that when dealing with what is invisible, we must always seek protection by our Angels, Teachers, or Guides, or whatever name with which you feel comfortable. These highly evolved Beings protect us from intrusion by other less-evolved Beings. It is important to ask for protection for ourselves and all our loved ones, including patients, students, and clients.

You now carry the Love energy. It is not welcomed by all. This can make you a disruptive presence. Therefore, ask for protection from any who might seek to hurt you or your loved ones.

In Meditation each day, ask for protection from any Beings, in sight or invisible, who might want to harm you or those you love and care for. Do this with each Meditation until it becomes a habit. Ask for protection before sleep for you and your loved ones. Ask that you continually be guided by Love in all situations, and at all times.

The New Message of Love
II. Journey to Love

Notes

WEEK 37

STEP 37

As you go more deeply into meditative states, you may begin to have more frequent experience. Consider many of the religions of your world. Information was revealed to certain people, recorded, and these historical events formed the basis of religion.

Religion has much value in inviting people into the spiritual path. It has value in supporting the family through life cycles and events. Some find they need more, and move further into meditation, their spiritual Path and Purpose, and become open to spiritual experience. Spiritual experience is not static. It appears uniquely to the person, and is often life-changing.

What experiences have you had that are beyond explanation? Do you know others also having spiritual experiences? The new spirituality is based more upon one's own experiences and less upon another's experience. Therefore, your experiences of spiritual guidance, sense or feeling of Presence, hearing or seeing beyond what the physical ear or eye can perceive, will be the catalyst for your life lived with spiritual experience and understanding.

In daily Meditation, ask for guidance and understanding. Ask to be centered, grounded, and able to receive. Ask to have anything that does not support your spiritual path to fall away.

The New Message of Love
II. Journey to Love

Notes

WEEK 38

The New Message of Love
II. Journey to Love

STEP 38

Review your notes regarding what you noticed about individuals without language. Now move this observation to groups of two or more people. The collective consciousness of a group will have an over-riding or prevailing intent. For example, a group of people may not individually intend to hurt another, but if the over-riding intention is to hurt or damage another, the group consciousness, often referred to as group-mentality, may prevail over individual differences.

In your encounters, and in any televised events, what did you detect as the stronger or prevailing intent? Note your observations. What can you extrapolate from this? Does Love motivate people in a direction? Does fear motivate them in another direction? Record your observations and thoughts regarding each.

In Meditation each day, ask to be aware of the intentions of groups of people. Ask to increase awareness of each person and each group. Did you notice some reluctant to follow the crowd? Did you note some appear to be fearful at opposing the group intention? Ask for protection from any individuals or groups that might harm you, or those you love and care for.

The New Message of Love
II. Journey to Love

Notes

WEEK 39   STEP 39

In your society, some people are given deference due to education, status, wealth, or experience. Consider those in positions of power throughout your life including teachers, religious leaders, physicians, business executives. Make a list of powerful people beginning from your childhood, with whom you interacted. Consider each slowly and carefully. Were there teachers who loved children, and others who did not? What was the impact of a special teacher who loved you? What was the impact of teacher whom you felt did not love you or another child in class? Do this activity over a two-week period, slowly examining each relationship. Consider your relationship with each of your parents separately. Write all that comes to mind.

In daily Meditation, ask for the ability to look at each relationship without judging yourself. Be completely honest about the impact each person had on your life, if any. Some will have had little impact; others may have brought joy or pain, self-confidence or lack of it.

Send love to each person, and thank them for the lesson learned.

The New Message of Love
II. Journey to Love

Notes

WEEK 40   STEP 40

Continue Step 39 all week. With each person you gained, or you lost, or both. Consider each person and write what was lost or gained next to each. Give yourself permission to be honest, as this is not to hurt another, but to recognize power in relationships, and to heal losses.

In Meditation each day, give thanks for those lessons learned, positive and negative. Ask to forgive them, as most were not aware of their power to hurt you. Ask for healing of the wounds you still carry. Give thanks that you now recognize great power of influence, pain, and positive impact. Ask, through Love, to be a positive influence for love in the world. Ask to be a Channel of Love and Peace through eternity.

The New Message of Love
II. Journey to Love

Notes

WEEK 41   STEP 41

Review your relationships over your lifetime in which you had power over another. In childhood relationships, in school relationships, in personal family and business relationships, consider your power. What message do you want to convey to others? What do you want to contribute to the world? Meditate for 1-2 minutes, then write whatever contemplations and guidance you receive.

In Meditation daily, give thanks for your new awareness, understandings, and opportunities. Ask for blessings for all of your personal relationships. Ask that all that cannot support you, fall away. Ask that you be able to release them with love.

The New Message of Love
II. Journey to Love

Notes

WEEK 42 STEP 42

Each day this week, write: "What do You want me to do?" Write the response.

In Meditation each day, ask for Love's will for your life. Ask to be purified that you might be a Channel of Love and Peace through eternity.

The New Message of Love
II. Journey to Love

Notes

WEEK 43   STEP 43

Just as there is much diversity in your world, there is much diversity in the world that you are unable to see. Beings exist at every level and vibration. They also exist in a body on many planetary bodies, many of which remain yet unseen or unknown. Your intention is to navigate safely through the seen and unseen to fulfill your purpose. Your purpose is to serve on earth. Your purpose also is to assist in the evolution that is occurring.

Many have visited and continue to visit your planet. Those visitations will continue to increase until there is mixing of humans and non-humans. Communication through telepathic means will be essential. As you learn, and become more adept and more capable of expanded communication, so are other Beings. Many non-human beings are already capable of telepathy, and know your thoughts as well as intentions. Therefore, the following Steps will be to increase your telepathic abilities.

In Meditation daily, ask that you become more aware of others' thoughts and intentions. Use the skills you developed in previous Steps to receive guidance, and enhance your ability to be more aware of people and animals around you. Do they elicit Love or Fear in you? Ask that they elicit only Love from you.

Notes

WEEK 44   STEP 44

The remainder of this curriculum will provide you with the skills necessary to safely evolve. Change is constant now in your world. Whether or not you can perceive it, your world is constantly changing in all areas: climate, politics, geography, technology, communication, and energy. Therefore, you will need to:

1) Be centered

2) Be aware of change within

3) Be aware of outside change

4) Develop new skills for managing and/or navigating change

5) Employ new skills as needed

As you meditate daily, ask: "What do You want me to do? Help me to hear, see, feel, understand that which can only be known intuitively. Open me to new experiences. Guide my daily continuous development."

Ask: "In all situations and at all times, make me a channel of Your Love and Peace through eternity."

The New Message of Love
II. Journey to Love

Notes

WEEK 45   STEP 45

The New Message of Love
II. Journey to Love

Practice becoming centered. Move to a quiet, accepting space, away from other's criticism and negativity. In a comfortable position, stand or sit with both feet firmly on the floor. Imagine a white light circling high about your head. As you focus, you imagine that circling white light descending slowly down to the center of the top of your head. As it descends, it picks up speed. As it moves downward, it moves through your body, through the head, neck, torso, and down your legs and into your feet. It pushes more strongly and quickly through your feet into the earth, where it continues to the inner earth's core. You are now in alignment with Love.

As you move forward each day this week, imagine that white light moving in concert with you, from far above your head, to the earth's core. Thus, you are centered, aligned with the Light of Love, and moving with protection through the world during all daily activities.

Repeat each day, moving in the conscious awareness that you move in Light at all times. At the end of each day, write whatever comes to you, whether observations, experiences, inspiration or any other thoughts. Repeat this entire process each day for one week.

The New Message of Love
II. Journey to Love

Notes

WEEK 46

STEP 46

You are now in the forty-sixth week of this year-long curriculum. How have you changed? How have others changed in response to you? What change has been easy? What change has been difficult? What change has been painful? What change has been joyful? What feels different? What seems different? Do you feel confident? Assured? Open to experience? Less judgmental? Less fearful?

Each day following meditation, write your thoughts, positive and negative, about these changes. Do not judge your responses. Simply write and let these thoughts be revealed to you.

The New Message of Love
II. Journey to Love

Notes

WEEK 47 — STEP 47

Each day in meditation, ask to have these changes in the outside world since you began this curriculum revealed to you. Who has changed? What has changed? Do you know why it changed? What is changing now? What will be some future changes?

Ask that these answers be revealed to you as you write. Repeat this activity from the beginning each day for six days. On the seventh day, summarize the items from all six lists into one complete list.

The New Message of Love
II. Journey to Love

Notes

WEEK 48   STEP 48

Trusting your own profound intuition is your biggest challenge. Even as you feel, think, even believe you know answers, your challenge will be to trust your own intuition to make wise and safe decisions.

Challenges will be presented to you this week in which you will need to make decisions without all of the information necessary. Use your profound intuition to make each decision that presents without adequate information. Write down each challenge, what you knew, what you didn't know, and what your intuition was telling you. What was the action you took? What were the consequences of the action? What was your intuition leading you to do? Was it the best choice? Did you experience doubt? Do you feel it was the best decision? Do this activity daily after saying the following in Meditation:

"I desire to learn the skills needed to navigate the world safely, even when I have inadequate information for a decision. Help me to learn to listen and follow wisely my profound intuition in all instances. Keep me safe in a confusing, changing world. Make me a channel of Your Love and Peace through eternity."

At the end of each day, review all consequential decisions you made. List each decision. Next to each decision, write Y for yes, and N for no. Did I rely upon intuition to make this decision? Knowing what I know now, would I make the same decision again? Why? Why not?

Repeat this activity at the end of each day, beginning with Meditation, and incorporating the following words:

"Make me a channel of Your Peace and Love through eternity. Guide me safely through each day and each situation presented. Help me to see, hear, feel, and know internally. Guide me in all decisions, that I may one day guide others safely through the evolution that is occurring."

The New Message of Love
II. Journey to Love

The New Message of Love
II. Journey to Love

Notes

WEEK 49   STEP 49

Practice for each of the next seven days what you know about each person on your path that day. Begin by listing each person, by name or description, on a page. Next to each one, write several comments about your perception of the person using only your intuition. (It is not necessary to record what you already knew or what they told you directly.)

At the end of each day, check to be sure that you were not responding due to bias. Note where you felt safe or afraid. Note any thoughts about the person that occurred when with the person, after parting from the person, and now reflection. What do you know intuitively that you did not know before?

Do this daily for 7 days, following Meditation. In prayer ask, "What do You want me to know about this person that can only be known intuitively?" Write the response.

As you go through the week, you will have several encounters with others. Some will be brief; some extended. Some will be with people well-known to you; others may

be complete strangers.

In each situation, you will first realize new information using your skills of seeing, hearing, feeling, and intuiting. What do you know that is new? How did that new information influence your decisions? How did your decisions influence each interaction?

After you make a list of each person, write your responses to the above questions following their name. Leave plenty of space for responses as you now know much more intuitively about each.

The New Message of Love
II. Journey to Love

The New Message of Love
II. Journey to Love

Notes

WEEK 50   STEP 50

Your profound intuition about a person or situation can be greatly altered by your fears, including biases, and your preferences. It is essential be become objective in order to truly perceive what is really occurring. If you are afraid of certain people due to learned bias or past experience, recognize that bias or fear, and then mentally move away from it.

In other situations, or with certain people, you may desire a particular outcome. If you cannot recognize, and then step away from, that desire or preference, you will not be able to intuit objectively.

Consider mistakes you have made when relying upon your intuition. Did you deeply desire a certain outcome (such as, return to health in the body)? Did you have fear, such as prejudice due to race or religion? Did these fears or preferences cause you to be unable to objectively understand your own intuition? What was the mistake you made? What was the outcome?

Consciously review your intuition-based decisions each day beginning with this prayer in Meditation: *"Help me to learn to receive information intuitively that can safely guide me, and others, through the evolution that is occurring."*

Review your notes from Lessons 42-49. Each day write down the first 5 thoughts that come to you by asking: "What are the 5 things I learned today after reviewing lessons 42-49?"

Repeat for seven days, beginning each Meditation with, *"What do You want me to know?"*

The New Message of Love
II. Journey to Love

Notes

Week 51   Step 51

This is an intense and productive Journey to Love that prepares you to navigate the changes you are facing, and will face. This preparation has been given to the world through Our messenger named Moriah. As you have taken each Step, the Lesson was prepared specifically for you. It is now time for you to move forward, supported by those relationships that are able to provide support; supported by the Teachers of Love who developed and shared this Preparation, and supported by Love. You will need to depend upon this support in all situations. Therefore, this week is devoted only to summoning and awareness of Presence.

In daily Meditation, ask that your Teacher Guides be present with you. Call them the name that has been given to you, or that feels right. You may also call upon the Teachers of Love. You are never alone.

After each Meditation, write whatever thoughts come to you. Write without judgment. Allow your thoughts to flow. Stop writing when the flow of words has stopped.

The New Message of Love
II. Journey to Love

Notes

The New Message of Love
II. Journey to Love

WEEK 52   STEP 52

This week, at all times, be grateful. List all that you are grateful for, beginning with the gift of life. Include family, friends, Guides/Teachers, experiences, and all with which your life is blessed.

Begin each daily Meditation with an expression of gratitude. Make a list of all you are grateful for that you can keep with you at all times. Refer to this list at the beginning of each hour you are awake for the next 7 days. You are developing the essential practice of living in gratitude.

"We, the Teachers of Love, are grateful for your openness and acceptance of this Preparation, Journey to Love. May it bless your life with direction, safety, peace and love."

The New Message of Love
II. Journey to Love

Notes

DEDICATION

You are a Channel for Peace and Love through eternity. But, first you must Love. Love is of God. Love is God in Action. Love is Energy. Love is Force. Love moves ever forward, touching and gathering those who would respond. Think not that Love is for your own pleasure. It is for the returning of all to God. Therefore, let not your desire for pleasure be that which moves you forward. Allow Love to be the invitation to the feast. You are the manna for God. It is only when you give yourself completely as the sacrifice, that Love can be given to the world. Let all your life be a prayer that God will make you worthy of this sacrifice. For He sacrifices only those who are worthy and gives only to those who would receive.

Be not afraid, for sacrifice is the final union with God and none can take away its Joy!

Book III.

The Healing Journey

The New Message of Love
III. The Healing Journey

Contents

Introduction to The Healing Journey	403
The Healing Journey	411
Bringing It All Together	413
Open to Healing	417
Your Healing Journey Reflections	419
A New Paradigm of Spirituality	461
Our Healing Journey	463
Life is not an Empty Slate	466
Healing of the Body Requires Healing of the Mind	469
Universal Energy for Healing	470
What is Healing?	473
Moriah's Healing Journey	474
Benediction	490
My Healing Journey	493

The New Message of Love
III. The Healing Journey

Introduction

It is a most difficult task to persuade other humans of the need to prepare. This Preparation from God is revealed as Humanity goes more deeply into the universal evolution required to move from a global tribal community, to one of the communities of the greater universe. We will explain….

Your people want to know why. Why is the climate changing radically? Why do I feel so ungrounded? Why do I want to escape other humans? Why are many seeking refuge and family with pets? Why do some hold onto outdated beliefs, both religious and scientific? Why do people try to recreate or destroy childhood memories? Why are some people risking life and career to warn and assist others? Why is the world becoming more dangerous? What can I hold onto? What will make me feel centered and whole? What will ground and strengthen me? Why do so many live with increasing anxiety? What are the "new" diseases? Why is pain increasing? Why are people choosing not to live, and not to bring children into the world? Why is there such disparity of resources? Why is trust crumbling in all areas? What can we do?

At times of great change, people struggle to maintain equilibrium. They find it very challenging to move forward, and they have less patience for self and others.

People need an anchor, even more so during great turbulence of change. It is even more challenging as trust fades in the institutions which have signaled stability: homes, families, government, schools, religion.

As those foundations are shaken, new anchors must be developed to assist during this great evolutionary disturbance.

Consider this: Imagine that you live for many years on a small island. You are the only human. Your life isn't easy, but it is predictable. The day is spent doing what is necessary to survive. You hunt and prepare food. You watch out for hungry predators. You seek and make shelter. Your days are consumed by activities needed to live.

One day, other human visitors arrive. They don't look like you. In fact, you don't really know how you look to others, but they are strange. They make unintelligible noises to you. They have different habits. And you do not know if they came as friends, or predators.

This is the condition now for Humanity. Humans have believed that they are alone in the universe. Now it has become clear to many that being alone was only an illusion, based upon one's experience. Humans, for all their individual differences, look much alike, yet humans have erected walls to isolate themselves from each other. They have built walls of social class, geographical boundaries, and beliefs. As these walls are brought down, humanity is preparing for a New World in which humans are but one group of intelligent life.

Like the one person on an island encountering reality-shattering proof that he is not alone, Humanity, too, is facing mounting evidence that Others have come and continue to come here. The Others are curious, and they are exploring. They have obtained samples of Human DNA for their own purposes. Their purposes are survival, and evolution. They have moved beyond their species identity, and come for many reasons. There will be no common language. Humans will need to rely upon instincts, long abandoned for more sophisticated communication.

Humans are not equally aware of the evolution that is occurring. Without awareness, they cling to superstition and dogma. As more humans "wake up" to the reality of this global, universal evolution, there will be much fear, disrupting violent behaviors, and philosophies of "live for now", or "escape the world". This is not necessary. A Preparation is given for the safe unification of our worlds, but Humanity must first learn this Preparation called, "The New Message of Love."

Humanity is on the threshold of an earth-shaking, paradigm-breaking, event. This event will re-write history as your people learn truth when they are able to clear their minds of dogmatic beliefs, and see what is really occurring. What has been, is, and will continue to occur is the exploration and unification of Humanity with the Other intelligences of the Universe. Indeed, much is occurring in sight that is still hidden because the human mind filters out that which does not fit its paradigm of reality. We will explain.

A child is born with an open, inquisitive mind. At birth, there are new experiences such as seeing, feeling touch, adjusting to temperature fluctuations, hearing sounds beyond the sounds experienced in utero, and tasting and consuming food. The child is making connections with these experiences: I like this. I don't like that. Hunger, loneliness, and eventually fear enter the child's

consciousness. The baby takes in new information and its brain draws conclusions.

As the child develops, it is aware of the values of the parents and caregivers. Some behaviors are regarded as good;

others are forbidden. The child's own value system is simultaneously developing, and forming judgments: right, wrong, good, bad, acceptable, unacceptable, delicious, unpleasant.

As the development continues, the child is exposed to lessons that reveal the parents' beliefs. Many children attend and belong to a specific religion whose values are acceptable to the parents. Thus, the child's concept of reality is being developed. This is a simple, yet effective, way to look at how a person develops over time into a youth, and then an adult. If during this time only current paradigms (generally accepted beliefs) are introduced or experienced, the person's view of reality, or the way it is, is perhaps unquestioning. It now forms the foundation upon which life choices are made.

Unexamined, unquestioned "reality" is the widely accepted view of what exists. When events, or experiences, or new information challenge the person's paradigm of reality, growth begins. However, this growth may take time and many more experiences before the person sheds his belief system in confusion.

Here is where struggles and challenges often create difficult situations which may lead to destructive behaviors, or may develop into new philosophies and beliefs.

It is at this point that the adult child separates from the parental beliefs to move onto a path of discovery. This is a challenging time for families, often wrought with misunderstandings, feelings of rejection, and accusations of lack of appreciation. Some people may change careers. Some marriages may not withstand the changes that the "developing" person may make. Communication often suffers, even when dialogue is continued and pressed. Families suffer as the changes may divide them. It can be a very painful and frightening, yet exciting, time. Each person continues to develop, if sometimes separately.

There are primarily two paradigms of reality that are causing great conflict within relationships at this time. There are people who have experienced, and continue to experience, paranormal events that do not fit the generally accepted view of reality. That reality is not yet open, but is opening to, metaphysical experiences such as seeing, hearing, feeling, and exhibiting abilities not developed by most humans. These people are generally not believed, and when they continue to speak on these metaphysical abilities and events, they may be condemned and shunned by society.

At this time, as the numbers have increased of those with psychic abilities and experiences of consciousness that cannot be explained by the current paradigm of reality, these people are uniting. People find safety and solace in the company of others having these experiences, yet are often shunned by family, friends, and work associates. Many hide their knowledge until they find an "appropriate" time to "come out of the closet." The price one pays varies, but many must walk away from those who no longer can accept them.

The great divide in your world at this time is not political and partisan. The divide is between those who still accept the general view of reality, and those who cannot accept this view but have a more inclusive view. Those with new open paradigms of reality are your new leaders. They do not necessarily have political power, but they have great political influence.

Your institutions are based upon the generally accepted view of reality. It is what they teach. It is what they stand for. They are being challenged, not by other humans or countries; they are being challenged by new beliefs and paradigms of reality. As this "new" paradigm develops which incorporates all the experiences: UFO's, Others (aliens), psychic abilities, channeling, direct divine guidance, visitations, teleportation, remote viewing, and ways of knowing through intuition, the institutions are challenged. When the tipping point is reached, the institutions will crumble. Already that is occurring. Traditional education, religions, medicine, science, psychology, parenting, governmental and political leadership are all impacted by lack of acceptance. Each is questioned, challenged, and often rejected. However, the dilemmas for those who no longer accept the current paradigm is, "Where do I belong?"

If one cannot teach what is required by the curriculum. If one can no longer limit medical treatment options to those within a current medical paradigm. If one no longer maintains a perception of the Creator that one was taught. If one no longer is accepted by friends and family—one is bereft of a sense of belonging, and thus protection. One must find new friends, belief systems, medical treatments, educational curriculums, and methods of parenting. And one may be forced to make these necessary changes while still responsible for growing families.

That's why New World Empowerment Ministries was born. That's why Moriah is bringing a Preparation called, "The New Message of Love." That's why this ministry is designed to minister to All Beings, to accept people of all abilities and beliefs, and to help people understand and practice the Preparation for this New World.

You, whose reality can include the unexplained, will be called upon to assist in this evolutionary change. The New World moves beyond the static paradigm of the past, and creates a new paradigm that continually expands with new information and awareness.

If you are reading this, it may be because you have heard, seen, or experienced that which cannot be true in the old paradigm of reality. If so, please continue to find refuge and solace in knowing that you are not alone, and you are needed to help humanity prepare for the integrations of many worlds and universes. We are not at the beginning, but we are far from the end. Join us as we prepare for the New World through the Preparation, "The New Message of Love", given to Humanity through Moriah. This Message provides us with the skills essential to safely navigate the new and coming challenges.

The New Message of Love
III. The Healing Journey

The Healing Journey

All life is about healing of the separation from Love, and the return of the soul to wholeness, or unity with the Godhead. Human life is about seeing oneself as separate, and taking a path to reach this state of union. Many are unable to do so. They fall away in lives of recklessness, shallowness, and living in the spotlight while simultaneously hiding in the shadows. They will join in another lifetime.

Life is about choices. One may choose to join and return Home, to the Source from which one came. One may also choose to remain separate. Thus, the Invitation to Love is the invitation to return to union with one's Source. Journey to Love is the soul's curriculum for joining. Life is The Healing Journey, and encompasses all of the roadblocks, twists, turns, rising and falling that are part of each life.

Life appears chaotic. In reality, it is a system of blocks and victories. Those steps that one overcomes are victories. Those that remain unaccomplished or unhealed are blockages. Therefore, the challenge of one's assignment on the earth-plane is to discover one's uniqueness and separation; decide whether to accept the Invitation to Love, and thereby begin the Journey to Love; and to encounter each challenge as it presents itself. One can use each challenge to propel one to victory, or to allow oneself to become stuck, and unable to go forward. In each life, the opportunity to surrender one's life to a greater power is given. The evidence of one's choice can be seen by their behavior.

You have seen those who encounter multiple challenges: sickness, loss, disability, and yet are able to say that it is their relationship with God, or Love, that moves them forward.

You have seen those lost to drugs, risky behaviors, and the dark side of Humanity. Alone, they feel abandoned. Desperate, yet unable or unwilling to surrender, they make choices that are detrimental to themselves and others. Their blatant disregard for the pain they cause drives them deeper into addiction and denial. Unless an intervention effectively convinces them to abandon their self-destructive path, they fall away into further illness and denial.

At this time, Humanity is facing a crisis of this decision, and its resulting losses. It is clear that an intervention that awakens Humanity is on the horizon.

Bringing It All Together

The Healing Journey begins by recognizing that we are all One, and the barriers that divide us are caused by our own creations. Humans created language. Within that language system, we created divisions, categories, and endless exceptions or explanations to further describe those categories. Take the word Love. There is Love meaning Universal Energy Source from which we all sprang, and to which we shall all return. There is the meaning of love as it refers to parents, spouses, partners, friends, offspring, pets, and continues, to lesser degrees, to those for whom we feel slight affection. There is romantic love, and there is acquired love. There is love between a parent and child which can be severed in the body, but never severed from beyond.

Love is an Energy. It moves from person to person, uniting them at any of a variety of levels. That is the distinction that was previously described, but also refers to a greater love for Humanity. There is love of country, which is the principle upon which that boundary-contained mass of land and people exist. There is love of ideas and philosophies, and there is love of religion.

Some people have said that religion has caused more wars than any other reason. That is problematic, as religion is constructed to teach people to, by whatever path, follow Love. The great spiritual Teachers and Leaders followed Love and urged their followers to do the same. Yet, it is the very principle upon which religion is founded that gets lost when people judge one another as "less than" due to affiliation.

Language is often the great divider, and although efforts have been, and are continually made, to articulate meaning even more precisely, words can divide. For this purpose, we shall look at the life of Jesus the Christ.

Jesus was unique because he was both human and divine. In his divinity he could see the frailty of man, and forgive weaknesses and poor decisions. He understood human ego needs for gratification, recognition, and power. He taught that Love was mightier than any ego needs, and challenged followers to follow Love. He did not ask to be put on a pedestal and worshipped. He asked his Disciples to follow him, and do as he did: heal the sick, raise the dead, love one's enemy. When the divide he caused became unbearable to some, he was destroyed in order to destroy his Message. However, the Message survived and thrived.

It is possible that the Message has become interpreted and enshrined in such a way as to make it difficult, perhaps impossible, for followers to grow. As we have witnessed so many exiting the construct of Christianity, it appears often that it is done because the individual chooses to grow and allow for more direct spiritual experience. What if people could grow and develop through these established great religions, but see them as occurring within the necessary time periods, while recognizing that spiritual infusion into our world has continued and today is even magnified? People are reporting evolution of consciousness in all areas of life. Electronic communications allow people of diverse faiths to communicate, and that communication is at times increasing the divides, but often helping us to acknowledge our common Humanity, and our need to reach toward unity with God, Love, Source, Universal Energy, Higher Power, or by whatever name you prefer. It is the emptiness in one's heart that causes one to reach for more, and it is Love that fills this vacuum in the soul.

If we choose another word, Consciousness, by which we express the desire for and subsequent reaching that appears to occur at some point in each life, we have a common word for a familiar experience. If we think of consciousness as something akin to water level, we can see in very simple terms how it works. All Humanity is within this sea of Consciousness. It expands and contracts constantly. As individuals, through Love-connection, or God-connection, raise their individual consciousness, it raises all. Conversely, as one follows one's lowest motives, all are affected. Thus, the level of Consciousness is fluid, and can become somewhat volatile.

Consider the effects of an act of violence. The anger it evokes causes the individual to first want retaliation. Retaliation may bring satisfaction to some, but it also increases the overall violence, which affects the level of Consciousness. As many turn to prayer for assistance and caring for one another, the level of Consciousness then begins to rise. The level of Human Consciousness is the total of all individual consciousness. Thus, in history, when Human Consciousness is low, an intermediary Spiritual Being appears to lead Humanity out of that darkness. This has happened repeatedly in history, and has led to many great religions. However, in spite of their teachings, once again the world is in darkness, with great challenges between light and darkness, good and evil. Which will prevail depends greatly on the direction of the level of our combined Consciousness.

Consider that humans, due to our own greed, callousness, and deceit, have created our world as it exists at this moment. If you are one who wants to move our world toward Love, you can assist by moving your own Consciousness toward Love. You can accept the Invitation to Love. You can do the spiritual practice called Journey to Love, and you can be part of The Healing Journey. As you make the decision to accept this Invitation to Love, and begin the daily curriculum of Journey to Love, you begin to raise your consciousness, which, in turn, begins to raise the entire Human Consciousness. That is why you hear spiritual leaders tell you that if you want to change the world, it is essential to first change yourself. The New Message of Love has come to show you how, to give you the way. *By taking this spiritual journey, you are at once affirming your religion by recognizing that it brought you to this point, and now you are able, with it as your firm foundation, to take the next step in your individual spiritual journey.*

A great religion is the initiator. You are now ready to begin the journey Home.

Much will go with you; much will fall away as you become this beautiful person bringing light to darkness, love to fear, and joy to emptiness. Your circumstances may not change, but you will change within your circumstances. And as you evolve, all that is needed will be provided. You are never alone.

Open to Healing

Healing is the acceptance of Universal Energy. It is the heart opening to allow this. It is the recognition that all of life is recorded in one's energy system. All recordings are attached to human emotions. All emotions are recorded in chakras. Therefore, when the chakra system becomes overloaded, illness occurs.

Humans exist within Universal Energy. It is around, over, and throughout them. Universal Energy is the environment in which all life exists. Therefore, when chakras become clogged or depleted, Universal energy can clear and fill the energy vortexes.

All food is energy. It is metabolized to become energy needed by the body. Thus, what is ingested is food for the body, and subsequently, the mind and soul. Therefore, the food energy taken in interacts with the body characteristics, and can itself promote health or dis-ease.

As you ascend the vibrational ladder, your physical needs change. Foods that are compatible with the vibrational level cause health and improved feeling physically, mentally, and emotionally. However, more dense foods must be released in order to allow the body optimal functioning. As you see others devoting their lives to their spiritual purpose, you may note that they have made dietary changes due to increased awareness of others' suffering, or increased suffering within their body-mind system.

As you move forward in Love energy, note all that supports your journey, and release all that no longer serves that purpose. As you progress, healing is essential so that the spirit is nourished and in turn desires service. Note those who are healing; you will see a new or renewed desire to serve.

Allow healing to occur. Release all that does not support your journey: food, activities, relationships, obligations, and beliefs. Healing will occur as you abandon self-defeating thoughts and actions. It is so ordained.

The New Message of Love
III. The Healing Journey

Your Healing Journey

REFLECTIONS

Reflective questions are provided here to assist you in **Your Healing Journey**. After a brief meditation, write your thoughts on the space provided following the question.

It is suggested that you keep a separate notebook available with you at all times to record healing thoughts as they come to you. And now, Your Healing Journey……

The New Message of Love
III. The Healing Journey

1. What have I learned in The New Message of Love that has added joy to my life?

2. What is my biggest challenge with The New Message of Love?

The New Message of Love
III. The Healing Journey

3. Who can assist me?

4. Who is having difficulty with my new choices?

5. Who can help?

6. How can I better use my time for spiritual practice?

7. What were once my dreams?

8. What happened to my dreams?

9. Where in my life do I feel most fulfilled?

10. What do I see that I want to improve?

11. What is my Spiritual Purpose?

12. Where can I find help with my Spiritual Purpose?

13. Do I see others working toward this Purpose?

14. What people or organizations can help me?

15. Does my primary relationship support my Spiritual Path?

16. Do my family members support my Path?

17. Do my friends support my Path?

18. Am I alone on my Path?

The New Message of Love
III. The Healing Journey

19. Who can help me?

The New Message of Love
III. The Healing Journey

20. Where can I find support?

21. Is my place of spiritual practice welcoming? Comfortable? Inspiring? Quiet?

22. What can I do to make my place of Spiritual Practice support me better?

23. When I am rejected, where can I turn?

The New Message of Love
III. The Healing Journey

24. Have I surrendered to Love?

25. Am I willing to surrender again?

26. Can I make an anniversary date of my surrender/commitment, and celebrate it annually? What is my date?

The New Message of Love
III. The Healing Journey

27. Is there something I can wear as a symbol of my Commitment to Love?

28. Am I willing to invite others to join me?

The New Message of Love
III. The Healing Journey

29. Who can join me?

30. Who is unable to join?

31. Can I find the strength to deal with rejection?

32. Can I find the strength to keep on going?

33. What resources do I need?

34. Do I believe that "what is needed will be provided"?

35. I commit to my Purpose and Calling in the world.

The New Message of Love
III. The Healing Journey

36. I surrender my life to Love.

The New Message of Love
III. The Healing Journey

37. I will go where I am called.

38. I will invite others:

The New Message of Love
III. The Healing Journey

39. Love will sustain and guide me.

40. I am never alone.

The New Message of Love
III. The Healing Journey

A New Paradigm of Spirituality

Healing comes to us when we least expect it. While we wait, after seeking healing, events and people create new opportunities. When one has been hurt or rejected, the pain of rejection is healed when one accepts oneself as more important that the judgments of others.

The life you are living now sits on top of the experiences of previous lifetimes in a body. The shame or pain one feels in this lifetime is actually a re-wounding of wounds from previous lifetimes.

Pain is universal, as Love is universal. Fear and its progeny (doubt, uncertainty, and projection of negative emotions) follow pain of rejection. Physical un-ease in the body can sometimes be related to accidents or illness in previous lives. In other words, life in the body is a continuum. That is why when one achieves healing in one lifetime, similar wounding from previous lifetimes is also healed.

Love is an energy that sears through dis-ease, interrupting the status quo, and lancing the poisonous negativity within. It is as if Love lances the negative stored energy, opening it to burst out of its encapsulation, and drain. Once negative energy is drained, one is now ready to fill the empty space left behind with Love energy.

Unexplained actions or events can also create the opportunity for healing rigidity. As one holds firmly to the religious teachings from youth, one will have experiences that directly negate a part of that prior teaching. This challenge to one's faith is most confounding. At first, one is often able to explain away, deny, or deny the implications of the experiences. However, memories of the experience, or more experiences, can belabor the issue, causing much internal disruption for the person. This internal conflict continues, often becoming more insistent and uncomfortable, until one experiences a shift in one's perspective, a change in one's belief paradigm.

Sometimes at this point, the person leaves organized religion, or searches other established religions. This becomes a spiritual quest for truth. Internal conflict may continue until one realizes that "reality" is more than beliefs framed in an unyielding structure. Now one's true journey has begun. It may take one to new heights of understanding, or, may lead one away from spirituality and religion as disillusionment overtakes the person.

At this juncture, new explanations are often sought. It can be a period of great personal growth. It can also leave one bitter at the world and at those finding comfort in their new understandings. This is the choice one makes. One either accepts Love in all its forms, and moves forward on one's healing journey, or one remains stagnant until another lifetime and invitation are received. Thus, the healing journey is life, healing is available, yet free will requires the person to choose internally which he or she will follow.

Allow yourself to be open to new experiences. Allow an open and personal interpretation of these experiences. Experiences are designed to teach us what we need to learn. All new learning about Love moves one forward on one's path. And so it is.

Our Healing Journey

In the beginning we awoke in the womb. Already we were learning and preparing for a life of service. Our destiny was determined by our parents, and the environment into which we would enter the world was designed and waiting. Already a religion, or none, was part of our learning tree. Already much was determined regarding our status, access, health, and predetermined expectations from family.

We learned before birth to experience sound, pain, comfort, security, or lack of security. We absorbed into our consciousness the relationship of our parents to one another, and knew before birth if our existence was welcomed.

Already we knew experiences of parental and other anxiety. We carried memories from other lives and before birth. We were an awakening consciousness with memories of lives and lessons. We began where we left off: some lessons learned; some to be learned.

We brought our unique consciousness into a waiting world. It had experienced death and new life before. Some relationships were renewed; others left for yet another lifetime. Life on a continuum. And so it was.

With pre-natal activity and post-natal responses, we gained, and brought forward, wounds. Those wounds unhealed from previous lifetimes appeared in new symptoms and configurations. We might have experienced colic, pain, feeling of rejection, aloneness, insecurity, instability, or health and ability to thrive challenges. The consequences of these early experiences, themselves, a result of prior lifetimes, created chaos for many, and may have contributed to our sense of being welcome in the world we had just entered.

Lessons of life begin early. Acceptance or rejection; Love or absence of love; Pain or comfort; Ease or dis-ease; Life as a flow or life with challenges and interruptions. All of this was recorded in consciousness. All of this, and subsequent lessons, were healed, or recorded within the body-mind-spirit.

Upon reaching adulthood, and sometimes before, these recordings in our mind-body-spirit may become troublesome, and signal a need for healing. All healing of the body follows healing of the spirit. All healing of the mind accelerates this healing. Thus, healing of the mind-body-spirit is required for these recordings of pain, abuse, or uncaring, to be erased.

Healing is a life-long journey, and not a single destination. Healing occurs in waves when one is ready. As old emotions emerge, they can be healed. As the healing occurs and the person regains equilibrium, the next wave is prepared. Therefore, healing of the mind-body-spirit is lifelong. New wounds that remain unhealed become apparent in the next generation. That is why you may see generations of abuse within a family. It continues until one says, "Enough!" And the healing begins.

When lives are short, it is tragic for families and loved ones. Humans cannot see the bigger Plan, and understand that what was needed was accomplished within this short time-frame.

All humans experience physical and emotional pain. It is the healing of these prior, and present, injuries that is the lesson of that lifetime. It may come in the form of loss, injury, illness, and many variations of these, but healing these challenges through

The New Message of Love
III. The Healing Journey

Love energy is the lesson. One cannot heal addiction, for example, by simply removing the addict from the substance. All of the emotional injury and confusion that preceded the addiction still exist. Therefore, true healing of addiction requires acceptance of Love energy to allow all of the wounds—mental, emotional, and physical—to heal. It is lack of Love that leads to addiction, and it is acceptance of Love that leads back to health.

Life is not an Empty Slate

We enter into this lifetime carrying unhealed wounds from previous lifetimes. Each lifetime is an opportunity to heal wounds from the past and the present. Indeed, wounds in the present are in reality re-woundings in need of healing.

Life is a series of events. Each lifetime contains joy and sorrow, pain and relief, lies and truths. It is the person who must learn what is right and true, and what is only masked as truth.

A baby learns, or is unable to learn, trust. Trust is stability. It sets up expectations for repetition. If one experiences another as trustworthy, it creates the expectation that the other may be trusted again. In the event that trust is broken, the sense of having been betrayed can be devastating.

When one looks in the mirror, one sees oneself. After many repetitions, one expects to see oneself as he or she has previously appeared. Accidents and illness can change one's appearance and the way that one sees oneself. That betrayal may send one seeking for new or improved identity. The soul craves reliability and must adjust for change. Thus, illness requires healing, not only of the body, but also the mind and emotions.

The location of each lifetime is carefully prepared and selected for the lessons of that lifetime. A lifetime of abundance may be followed by a lifetime of simplicity or even scarcity. This teaches the value of the soul as being complete without the trappings of one's culture.

Therefore, you may see people who seem to have acquired little in the physical world, yet who have character and personality full of love, caring and joy.

You may see others who have much in the way of comfort and society's definition of success, yet are depressed and angry. They are often empty, and lacking the connection to Love that brings true fulfillment. Unless they are able to be vulnerable and surrender their lives to Love, they will continue their own self-destruction. This can be most upsetting to family and friends who know how to relieve their pain, but cannot penetrate the walls built to retain their misery. Many will only heal in a future lifetime.

Love heals, and is available to all who seek it and open themselves to acceptance. Denial of Love continues one on an eventual desperate track. It is each person's right to choose. Free will means that one may accept or reject Love. Lack of Love leads to the deterioration of the mind-body, and recovery may not occur in the present lifetime.

When one continues to deny Love energy, their deterioration affects the family and friend network meant to support each person. It creates pain for each person to heal. Therefore, that person becomes toxic to all who surround them. Those who are pained must then heal their wounds, sometimes in spite of the lack of healing in the one who refuses Love. Therefore, addictions and destructive behaviors affect the family and friend system, creating pain and suffering that often require a lifetime of Love and healing.

Humans are interconnected. Once joined in relationship, the actions of one affect all others. Therefore, destruction of oneself or others creates a climate of distrust and pain that requires time and Love energy to heal.

Healing of the Body Requires Healing of the Mind.

Your Healers work to diffuse painful memories in the emotional and mental bodies. Energy accrues in the body that causes one to feel unwell. Often the symptoms are mild or sporadic at first, but if not attended to, become more severe. Accumulation of negative energies in the body over time creates an unwell condition leading to disease. Disease is the un-wellness of the mind-emotional bodies made manifest.

Dis-ease of the mental-emotional body has many manifestations. It can occur in a part of the body often related to the unease. Anxiety is caused by living in a potential future that is painful, or dangerous. It is not living in the present moment. Dis-ease of the joint is caused by painful memories associated with previous accidents, illness, or abuse. In general, the negative energy forms in the location associated with the memory. This is not always the case, but is a clue to the Healer when attempting to dissipate negative energy, thereby preventing illness.

When you entered the world, you came with a history from previous incarnations. In each incarnation, if the opportunity to heal is not seized and accomplished, the negative patterns follow into succeeding incarnations. Thus, the Invitation to Love is given in each incarnation, offering the opportunity for healing to occur.

In the beginning there was energy. It materialized into the universe as you understand it. Humans are but a micro-universe within the larger universe. All return to the Energy from which they came.

Universal Energy for Healing

The employment of Universal Energy for healing is in need of clarification. Your people may have good intentions for the well-being of another, yet they have not mastered this gift.

Universal energy is available to all, but few understand how to access it. People often ask: Is Energy good or evil? For what purpose can it be used? Is it possible to hurt another through the use of Universal Energy? How does it heal?

We are here to tell you that you are playing with Energy like a child with a toy. You know some of its power, but not how to use it safely and effectively. We will explain.

Universal Energy is the author and designer of the life of the Universe. This Universe is energy. You are energy. All that you perceive is energy. Life-energy is the movement of energy in all human life. That changes at the moment you call death. In actuality, death is the movement of life-energy from one universe into another.

Intention provides the direction and focus of energy. If it is being intentionally directed toward healing, the process will be accelerated, but not changed. In other words, if healing is to be within the body, the body will experience more rapid change. If healing is to be beyond the body, that process will also be expedited. In the latter, the person who is ill will begin having experiences in preparation for this transition. Therefore, when you pray, do so in the absence of preference as you cannot control the outcome.

As humans advance in their understanding of healing with Universal Energy, they will be humbled by the recognition that life has endings and beginnings as part of the greater Plan.

Consider employing Universal Energy in other areas. It can remove internal blockages to one's success, provide guidance, and energize depleted physical condition. It can move one to be open to other opportunities. It can advise one whether to go forward, maintain, or retreat as a decision. It promotes personal effectiveness by assisting one to know whom to trust and whom to avoid.

Universal Energy is employed when we choose to see a "glass half full." It propels one in a positive direction, while focusing on the negative gives negative direction a boost.

Humans did not, do not, create energy. They cannot control Energy, however they can direct and focus it.

Moriah had such an experience. When she saw pairs of eyes during a meditative state of consciousness, she immediately recognized them as the "Grays", and commanded them to "Go Away!" They responded immediately and disappeared from view.

During energy Healing sessions with Moriah, clients reported out of body feelings and deep relaxation. Energy can be a tool to help others teleport to other levels of consciousness.

However, Universal Energy can be used to harm when used with negative intention. Moriah experienced energy abuse at the hands of a healer when in that moment of misunderstanding, the heart of the healer was filled with anger.

When employing or sending Universal Energy, recognize Its ability to cause disruption and change. Prayers for peace may be answered with a sword of truth before there can be peace. Evil thoughts manifest as horrors in individual lives and in all humanity. Thoughts have intention. Wishing evil on another contributes to the grief and sadness in your world. Change your thoughts, and behaviors, to those that are beneficial to self and others to help promote peace.

Unity promotes Universal Healing. Unity is the focused intentions of many toward the raising of humanity's vibration toward peace.

Human will is full of intentionality. Speak only of love and unity to evoke the highest vibration of Universal Energy.

What is Healing?

Healing is the final resolution with Love. It is the moment when all pain and suffering are released. It is a glorious moment when one awakens to newness all around. There is a familiarity of recognition of loved ones who previously passed. It is a time of unity and joy as one remembers one's Source and previous lifetimes.

After rest and renewal, new options are given as one's progress toward Love is assessed. One does not fail; one assesses lessons learned. Scenarios are provided for one's next adventure. One has many choices, and may choose to rest, or to move forward with new challenges. One chooses who will accompany one on the next journey. Other relationships are temporarily released until one may join again with "family" from previous lifetimes.

Those relationships that one will bring into one's next lifetime are chosen. Each will have a role. Lessons will be learned within this family unit that will move one farther on one's spiritual journey. The Invitation to Love will again be given. One will again choose whether to follow Love, or to attempt to manage one's life alone. Yet, in reality, one is never alone.

This cycle of lives continues for each Being until one has become one with One. It is a beautiful Plan as all will eventually join.

Do not allow fears of loss and death to overwhelm you. Love encompasses all life. All life is part of Universal Love. All will eventually join.

Moriah's Healing Journey

"Make me a channel of Your Love and Peace through eternity

......"

The New Message of Love
III. The Healing Journey

Healing begins with surrender ...

Healing Surrender

I surrender

    my will to Your Will
    my wants to Your Desire
    my understanding to Your Understanding
    my self to my Self
    my plans to the greater Plan
    my life to Your Service
    my heart to Your Love
    my fear to Your Peace.

    When the evening of my life is near
     I pray I will have completed my Purpose
    Your Purpose for my life.

Thank you for

    Life, Love, Family, Friends, Understanding, Purpose
    A Life to Live for You
    A Purpose to give for You.

    Love is all
    Love is the greater Plan
    Love is evolution
    Love is
    Remembering my first Experience
    Consoling me at a time of loss
    Letting me feel Your Energy
    Letting me know You were there

The New Message of Love
III. The Healing Journey

So many times I've felt You

> in the Energy that envelops me
> in the Voice that bids me there
> in the sights of nature
> and the warmth of Love

So many times

> Yet, in my humanity, I still doubt, I still fear, I still tremble
> But when I feel alone, You are there.
> Even more.
> Evermore

—Moriah

Healing Message of Love

The healing began, and I understood my pain.

Now I release my pain, and understand.

Forgiveness is the key to health and healing.

Anger at oneself is the source of all pain.

Release the anger, and healing begins.

Healing is a journey, not a destination.

Pain returns only to be released again.

When it returns, it is a warning

That there is still unfinished healing to do.

Face the challenge with trust and understanding

That you can face the anger once again.

Forgive the offender; forgive yourself.

It is the message of Love.

—Moriah

Healing Evolution

Trying to live in the now

    And not allow anxiety to overwhelm me.

Hoping for good news

    And prepared to go forward anyway.

Without a crystal ball

    We live hoping for the best.

If we attract what we emanate

    I am multiply blessed.

Whenever I think everything is cleared

    I get new lessons.

And so, I still evolve.

—Moriah

Healing My Soul

My heart is filled with gratitude as I reach inside for hidden resources lying in wait.

What I took for granted most of life is now my great challenge.

To walk again will mean inclusion in life's activities--gatherings, travel, speaking out, representing.

It's been a life lesson to learn that it's difficult to live life from the sidelines.

So many live lives of isolation: Those who

> are disabled of all ages
> have chronic pain and fatigue
> are mentally ill
> are living with addictions
> are not accepted by society
> have contagious or incurable diseases

So many watch and yearn, remembering when it was otherwise

> And wishing for more.

Now I will understand.

Whether I walk again, or not

> I will know

Because I'm one with them.

—Moriah

The New Message of Love
III. The Healing Journey

Heal Me

Heal me, I asked
    because I had not asked for myself.

Heal me, the Angels heard.
    Were They surprised?

Heal me, I prayed
    When I stopped thinking only of others.

Heal me, I cried
    Because I had waited so long.

Heal me, I moaned
    When life felt like "too much!"

Heal me, I sought
    When I accepted my vulnerability.

Heal me? I asked
    When I began to feel worthy.

Heal me, too, I prayed
    after asking for others.

Heal me, it echoed

The New Message of Love
III. The Healing Journey

    Across the universe so vast.

Heal me, it vibrated
    Jangling nerves unused to prayer.

Heal me? I asked
    Could it also be for me?

Heal me, I sighed
    When I finally understood.

Heal me, she exclaimed
    It pealed from rafters!

Heal me, she cried
    When pain of not changing became too great.

Heal me, she whispered
    Magnified by all the Angels round.

Heal me, she thought
    It's all that is left.

Heal me..........
    For I need Love.
Heal me.........
    If someone still cares.

The New Message of Love
III. The Healing Journey

Heal me.........
    If not too late.

Heal me..........
    And help me grow.

Heal me!
    She commanded to anyone who'd listen.

Heal me!
    She shouted to All out of sight.

Heal me! ....
    For I now I must do my Purpose.

Heal me! ....
    Until my last breath here is given.

Heal me.........
    For I am now completely Yours.

—Moriah

I Believe in Love

I believe

> in the inherent goodness of every person
> every person has a choice
> each person chooses to follow Love or fear
> each person receives increased energy to expand upon that choice

I believe

> that as Love energy fills one, choices become clear
> Love energy is magnified
> Love clears a path and casts all that is not in alignment
> as Love clears, old negativity surfaces

I believe

> that negativity is exposed for the purpose of healing
> that dark energy must come into the Light
> that as dark energy is exposed, physical manifestations present for healing
> that healing purifies one for service

I believe

> that Love requires continuous healing
> that Love clears out darkness to make room for Light
> that Light Beings lighten the world's darkness
> that Light exposes darkness where it hides

The New Message of Love
III. The Healing Journey

I believe

    that Light Beings serve Love
    that Love energy exposes darkness
    that dark energy can and will be healed
    that our planet is coming back into the Light

                                            —Moriah

The New Message of Love
III. The Healing Journey

At Peace

I am at Peace.
Life is not easy.
Friends and family are leaving
And they won't be coming back.

I am at Peace
'Though the world is rumbling
Expressing distaste
At bullies and fear.

I am at Peace
'Though I see so much pain
'Though I feel temporary
Even as I know I am not.

I am at Peace
'Though the diagnoses multiply
'Though resources dwindle
I am at Peace.

I accepted the Invitation to Love
And now only Love is enough.

Even pain is temporary.

—Moriah

The New Message of Love
III. The Healing Journey

Commitment

The Purification came

    and I am healed

Today I thank God

    Who has healed me

Today I realize

    that Love heals

Today I understand

    what I am to do

Today I once again

    Commit to my Purpose and Calling in the world

—Moriah

Gratitude for Being

I am thankful for my brain, the control center for my body. It allows me to think beautiful thoughts, enjoy scenic vistas, feel the wind in my hair and the sun on my skin.

I am thankful for my bosom. It has hugged and nursed my children, cushioned those in pain, and carried little ones from danger.

I am thankful for my arms. They add power to my piano music through the depths of my muscles. They have carried babies, puppies, and all of life's burdens. They have held the sick and reached out to the dying. They extend from my body to connect with others.

I am thankful for my lips. They have reassured children and elderly, taught in classrooms and auditoriums, carried messages of hope, and messages of peace.

I am thankful for my nose. It has carried my breath, bringing life to all my organs. It has warned of danger and sought food as energy. It precedes and guides, though is seldom recognized. I love my nose.

I am thankful for my hair. It provides protection from both heat and cold. It cradles me, yet expresses me. It can be carefree or uptight. It reflects my moods and presents a first impression.

I am thankful for my stomach. It receives food and converts it to energy that I may go, do, serve, enjoy. It makes life possible. I love my stomach.

I am thankful for my back. It has carried me through the years and miles of life. It has stood straight when attacked, bristled when appalled, and suffered under weights too painful to bear. It supports me without thought, takes abuse from daily chores, and then rests and recovers to carry me through another day.

I am thankful for my legs. They carry me where I desire, and rest to serve me another day. When tired and arthritic from years of use, they submit to treatments to help them continue. Always wanting to meet my needs, they keep moving even when they long to rest. I love my legs.

I am thankful for my fingers. They have endured years of exercises to be able to play beautiful music, yet caress a child or the ill or wounded. They send vital information to my brain, and protect me and others by doing so. They can recognize a fever or a fire, recoil from freezing, and brush aside cares. I love my fingers.

The New Message of Love
III. The Healing Journey

I am thankful for my feet and toes. They balance and carry me. They tolerate the pounding of weight for years, and are resilient for yet more. They take me to places only dreamed of by many. They feel the sand and water that make my heart thrill.

I am thankful for my heart. It beats thanklessly, taken for granted at every breath. It circulates my life blood, and carries that life to my whole body. Thank you, my heart. I love you most of all.

I am thankful for my Mind for it is far greater than my brain. It is my soul connection to the Divine, and life unending. It has carried me through many lifetimes in many places. It is all I truly am, my body simply a temporary manifestation. It contains all memories, and expands for more. It is I, yet greater than I. It is, and connects to the Divine of which I, as each of us, am a part. It is the beginning without end. It is consciousness. It is soul. It is higher self. It is who I truly am. It is who We each truly are.

And so, We continue, together.

--Moriah

Benediction

As you leave this place of serenity and solitude,
As you raise your hearts to Love,
    take with you the solemn commitment to devote yourselves-
        your lives, your efforts,
            your complete existence--to Love.

Love heals.
Love unites.
Love lifts.
Love guides.
Love joins all, who would accept, to everlasting love.

Think not that you are enjoined for your own purpose.
You are enjoined to bring forth Love into the world.
The world cries out for Love.
It is you, the spiritual sojourner, who must answer the call,
   and serve.

Let Love be your guide in all decisions.
Let Love light your way.
Let Love be all you seek,
    all you experience,
    all you express.
Now, and always.

        The Presence of the Teachers of Love is with us.

–Moriah

The New Message of Love
III. The Healing Journey

The New Message of Love
III. The Healing Journey

The New Message of Love
III. The Healing Journey

My Healing Journey

The New Message of Love
III. The Healing Journey

The New Message of Love
III. The Healing Journey

The New Message of Love
III. The Healing Journey

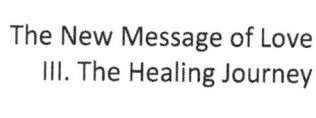

The New Message of Love
III. The Healing Journey

The New Message of Love
III. The Healing Journey

The New Message of Love
III. The Healing Journey

The New Message of Love
III. The Healing Journey

The New Message of Love
III. The Healing Journey

The beauty and greatness of love is without equal

It is timeless.

It is everlasting.

It will be with us through eternity.

And so it is.

--Moriah

Additional copies of **Christianity Transformed &**

The New Message of Love Books I-III

    Book I.   Invitation to Love
    Book II. Journey to Love
    Book III. The Healing Journey

are available on Amazon

To learn more about **The New Message of Love** visit:

    www.newworldempowerment.org
    www.humanempowerment.org
    www.thenewmessageoflove.com
    www.enterthenewworld.com
    www.newworldempowerment.com

Facebook pages:

    Moriah
    New World Empowerment Center
    New World Empowerment Ministries
    Moriah's New World Library
    International Institute For Human Empowerment

FB Group:

    The New Message of Love

INDEX
INSPIRATIONS

The Color of Love 17
In Their Voices 18
Jesus Was His Name 29
It's a New World 33
The New Revelation: Who Do You Say that I Am? 40
Surrender 52
Joy in the Pain 65
Acceptance 74
Assurance 88
Moriah's Healing Journey 474
  Healing Surrender 475
  Healing Message of Love 477
  Healing Evolution 478
  Healing My Soul 479
  Heal Me 480
  I Believe in Love 483
  At Peace 485
  Commitment 486
  Gratitude for Being 487
Benediction 488
The Beauty and Greatness of Love 502

Recognition

Photography – Sue Kidd Shipe, Ph.D.

Creative Design – Jody Morgenegg, CustomWebCare

Made in the USA
Middletown, DE
14 September 2023